PostgreSQL 17 QuickStart Pro

Add expertise around WAL processing, JSON table, IO performance, logical replication and index vacuuming

Tessa Vorin

Published by: GitforGits

Publisher: Sonal Dhandre

www.gitforgits.com

support@gitforgits.com

Printed in India

First Printing: October 2024

ISBN: 978-81-19177-84-4

Cover Design by: Kitten Publishing

Prologue

Hi, I'm Tessa Vorin, and I'm thrilled to present my new book, "PostgreSQL 17 QuickStart Pro"! It's packed with all the tips and tricks I've picked up along the way to help you get the most out of PostgreSQL 17 since its beta version became available. This book offers a fantastic, hands-on approach to learning all about PostgreSQL's newest features, optimization techniques, and high-availability solutions. It's perfect for database administrators of all experience levels!

I want you to feel like you're creating something truly special from the very beginning! I've used the incredible Titanic dataset as a consistent example throughout the chapters, and it's going to be a great way to illustrate the concepts we're covering! I'm so excited to show you how we'll use this real-world dataset to perform tasks you're likely to encounter in your daily work! We're going to dive right in and start by focusing on upgrading to PostgreSQL 17! I'll show you exactly how to upgrade your system in the best way possible, with absolutely no stone left unturned! If you're starting with version 15, you'll see exactly how to upgrade, validate the setup, and reconfigure everything so it's production-ready—and it's going to be amazing!

And now for something really exciting! We're going to go deep into cluster administration. I guarantee that you will understand the inner workings of the process and memory models that power PostgreSQL 17—and it's going to be a wild ride! I've also included some really practical examples for managing clusters, setting up multiple databases, and fine-tuning your configurations for peak performance. Role management and security have become absolutely vital components of database management, and so here, I demonstrate how to design permissions and manage users efficiently. We will also discuss row-level security, authentication mechanisms such as LDAP and SSL/TLS integration, and data compliance.

Another topic that I believe you should master is performance tuning. I'll walk you through analyzing query execution plans with EXPLAIN and EXPLAIN ANALYZE, allowing you to optimize queries based on the performance insights they provide. We will look at memory management, parallel queries, and configuration parameters such as work_mem and shared_buffers. If you've been tasked with improving performance, this section will provide immediate benefits that you can apply to your existing setup. I've also included a chapter on managing complex data types and also discussing important extensions such as pg_trgm and hstore, to handle text searches and key-value stores.

I also emphasize table partitioning, wherein I show you to create partitioned tables and manage them effectively using partition pruning and maintenance techniques. Finally, no PostgreSQL installation is complete without an effective backup and recovery strategy. I demonstrate how to perform physical and logical backups, automate them with BART, and, most importantly, use PITR to recover from accidental data loss or corruption.

Throughout this book, you will learn how to manage streaming replication, ensure high availability, and implement failover and switchover procedures to keep your databases up and running. In this, book, you will discover workable answers to common problems, regardless of whether you are managing databases in simple, localized settings or massive, enterprise-level empires.

Content

Preface

PostgreSQL 17 QuickStart Pro is the definitive hands-on, practical book for professionals at every level, from entry-level administrators to seasoned experts. It provides rapid learning and practical implementation of PostgreSQL 17, focusing on the latest features and best practices to effectively manage, configure, and optimize PostgreSQL databases—and it does so effectively.

The book begins by using the Titanic dataset to illustrate practical examples of upgrade strategies, post-upgrade validation, and database configuration. Next, it covers cluster administration, configuration settings, and performance tracking. You will master the management of permissions and roles through intricate role hierarchies, authentication methods, and security settings. Next, we'll optimize server performance, plan queries, and manage resources based on real performance data.

The next section dives deep into complicated data types, bulk data operations, advanced indexing methods, and the creation of triggers and functions, all with an emphasis on effective data management. Next, you will learn about table partitioning strategies, performing physical and logical backups, database restoration, and process automation using BART. We then move on to streaming replication, where we will configure, administer, and monitor replication to ensure optimal uptime. Finally, we will explore point-in-time recovery, which allows us to restore databases to specific points in time by replaying WAL logs. In short, this book will equip database administrators with the knowledge and skills to confidently handle PostgreSQL 17 databases.

In this book you will learn how to:

- Upgrade and configure PostgreSQL 17, including post-upgrade validation and configuration.
- Learn PostgreSQL architecture, memory models, and cluster management.
- Use hierarchical permissions, authentication, and security for advanced role management.
- Tune server performance with query planning, resource management, and configuration tuning.
- Effectively use PostgreSQL extensions, JSONB, and arrays.
- Optimize queries with GIN, GiST, and BRIN indexing.
- Master table partitioning for large dataset performance and scalability.
- Automate physical and logical backups and confidently restore databases.
- Manage PostgreSQL streaming replication for high availability and automatic failover.
- Restore data using WAL logs and Point-in-Time Recovery.

GitforGits

Prerequisites

As long as you are enthusiast to PostgreSQL and database administration career, every single update to PostgreSQL technology must be obssessed to you, and so this book too. If you are a DB professional, you must read this book.

Codes Usage

Are you in need of some helpful code examples to assist you in your programming and documentation? Look no further! Our book offers a wealth of supplemental material, including code examples and exercises.

Not only is this book here to aid you in getting your job done, but you have our permission to use the example code in your programs and documentation. However, please note that if you are reproducing a significant portion of the code, we do require you to contact us for permission.

But don't worry, using several chunks of code from this book in your program or answering a question by citing our book and quoting example code does not require permission. But if you do choose to give credit, an attribution typically includes the title, author, publisher, and ISBN. For example, "PostgreSQL 17 QuickStart Pro by Tessa Vorin".

If you are unsure whether your intended use of the code examples falls under fair use or the permissions outlined above, please do not hesitate to reach out to us at support@gitforgits.com.

We are happy to assist and clarify any concerns.

Acknowledgement

I owe a tremendous debt of gratitude to GitforGits, for their unflagging enthusiasm and wise counsel throughout the entire process of writing this book. Their knowledge and careful editing helped make sure the piece was useful for people of all reading levels and comprehension skills. In addition, I'd like to thank everyone involved in the publishing process for their efforts in making this book a reality. Their efforts, from copyediting to advertising, made the project what it is today.

Finally, I'd like to express my gratitude to everyone who has shown me unconditional love and encouragement throughout my life. Their support was crucial to the completion of this book. I appreciate your help with this endeavour and your continued interest in my career.

Chapter 1: Upgrading and Setting up PostgreSQL 17

Brief Overview

In this chapter, you'll learn how to upgrade an existing PostgreSQL installation to version 17 and create a sample database for hands-on exercises. The latest version of PostgreSQL, 17, has a number of improvements that make it more scalable, practical, and fast. To benefit from these enhancements, database administrators and engineers must first understand the upgrade process. We'll start with a look at the new features and improvements. You'll see how these changes can improve both day-to-day operations and advanced database tasks.

Next, we'll show you the best ways to upgrade to PostgreSQL 17. This section will show you how to plan an upgrade so that it runs smoothly and does not disrupt critical operations. We'll look at different upgrade methods, such as in-place and logical upgrades, and help you decide which is best for your current setup and workload. After discussing upgrade strategies, we will carry out the actual upgrade process. We will provide a detailed, step-by-step walkthrough of upgrading from an earlier version, addressing any potential issues that may arise along the way. I will ensure that your database remains fully functional and optimized after the upgrade. Finally, we will validate the upgrade to ensure that the database is completely functional and optimized.

What follows is an instruction on how to create the Titanic sample database. This database will be used to provide demonstrations throughout the book. You'll use PostgreSQL 17 features and techniques in a real-world scenario. The Titanic dataset provides a comprehensive example of PostgreSQL data management and querying. The subsequent chapters build upon it perfectly.

Overview of PostgreSQL 17

PostgreSQL has earned its reputation as one of the most reliable, flexible, and powerful open-source relational database systems available today. It is trusted by businesses of all sizes and industries, from startups to Fortune 500 companies, for its ability to handle a variety of complex data structures, advanced queries, and workloads with ease. From technology companies using it for real-time data analysis and transactional processing to data-heavy industries like finance, healthcare, and e-commerce, PostgreSQL empowers organizations to deliver robust, scalable, and highly available database solutions. It continues this tradition of empowering businesses by introducing key improvements in performance, scalability, security, and usability.

With the rapid growth of data and the increasing complexity of modern applications, the need for high-performance, efficient databases has never been more critical. PostgreSQL 17 addresses these needs with new features and optimizations aimed at enhancing performance, managing large datasets, simplifying backup and recovery, and improving high availability.

Key Enhancements

Incremental Backup Support

One of the standout features of PostgreSQL 17 is the introduction of **incremental backups**, a long-awaited enhancement for administrators managing large-scale databases. Traditional backups in PostgreSQL required full backups, which could be time-consuming and resource-intensive. Incremental backups address this by only backing up the data that has changed since the last backup, significantly reducing storage costs and recovery times. This is especially beneficial for enterprise environments that handle terabytes of data and where downtime can result in significant financial losses. This new capability, integrated directly into PostgreSQL's backup tooling, allows administrators to automate their backup strategies more efficiently.

PostgreSQL 17 also introduces the new **`pg_combinebackup`** utility, which facilitates the combination of base and incremental backups, further streamlining the backup restoration process. These enhancements mean that even in the case of a disaster recovery scenario, database administrators (DBAs) can restore critical systems quickly without the need for full system rebuilds, making PostgreSQL 17 an even more attractive choice for enterprise-level operations.

Performance Optimizations for Queries

Performance has always been a core strength of PostgreSQL, and version 17 takes this even further with optimizations in query execution, particularly for **Common Table Expressions (CTEs)** and **UNION queries**. In previous versions, PostgreSQL would materialize CTEs, leading to inefficiencies in certain complex queries. PostgreSQL 17 improves this by allowing the planner to inline CTEs, enabling better execution plans and faster query processing, especially for larger datasets.

Additionally, PostgreSQL 17 brings improvements in how it handles **`IN`** and **`EXISTS`** subqueries. These subqueries can now be pushed down to foreign data wrappers, resulting in faster query execution when querying remote data sources. This is especially useful in distributed database environments or when integrating external systems into PostgreSQL. Furthermore, the ability to leverage planner statistics in these scenarios enables more efficient use of system resources, making complex queries easier to manage even as data scales.

Enhanced Logical Replication

Another key feature is the improved **logical replication** capabilities, which greatly benefit high availability and disaster recovery setups. Logical replication, which allows for more granular control over data replication, has been enhanced to allow logical replication slots to failover without requiring re-synchronization of data. This improves failover time and reduces downtime, which is critical in environments where database availability is essential, such as financial services, e-commerce, and healthcare systems.

Furthermore, PostgreSQL 17 introduces the **`pg_createsubscriber`** tool, which simplifies the process of creating logical replication on a physical standby server. By allowing logical replication slots to be managed more flexibly, PostgreSQL ensures that DBAs can maintain high availability even in the most demanding scenarios. These enhancements also improve the ability to handle mixed workloads involving both physical and logical replication, providing greater flexibility in how databases are structured and managed across multiple servers.

JSON Enhancements and SQL/JSON Support

As JSON continues to be a popular format for handling semi-structured data, PostgreSQL 17 builds on its already robust support for JSON by introducing the **`JSON_TABLE`** feature. This feature allows JSON data to be converted into standard PostgreSQL tables, making it easier for developers and analysts to query JSON data using familiar SQL syntax. This advancement simplifies the integration of non-relational data into PostgreSQL, making it more versatile for applications that handle diverse data types.

Additionally, PostgreSQL 17 adds support for SQL/JSON constructor functions like **`JSON`**, **`JSON_SCALAR`**, and **`JSON_SERIALIZE`**, as well as query functions such as **`JSON_EXISTS`**, **`JSON_VALUE`**, and **`JSON_QUERY`**. These functions allow for more powerful querying and manipulation of JSON data, improving the developer experience and enabling more flexible data workflows.

Partitioning and Indexing Improvements

Partitioning has long been a powerful feature in PostgreSQL, allowing DBAs to manage large datasets more efficiently by splitting tables into smaller, more manageable pieces. In PostgreSQL 17, the partitioning system has been further enhanced, adding the ability to **split and merge partitions**. This adds greater flexibility in managing partitioned data, particularly in systems where data volume grows rapidly, such as time-series data or event logging.

In addition to partitioning, PostgreSQL 17 introduces **parallel index builds** for BRIN indexes, improving the performance of indexing operations on large datasets. This feature allows multiple processes to build indexes simultaneously, reducing the time required for index creation and maintenance. The improved index handling also extends to B-tree indexes, with PostgreSQL 17 offering better execution plans for queries involving **`IN`** clauses, further boosting performance for complex queries.

Impact of PostgreSQL 17 Upgrade on Existing Systems

The upgradation to PostgreSQL 17 involves more than just installing the new version; it requires careful consideration of the impact the new features and configurations may have on your existing systems. One significant change is the introduction of new configuration parameters that must be properly managed to take full advantage of PostgreSQL 17's enhancements. For example, the new **incremental backup feature** requires configuring the backup strategy and storage to support incremental backups and their corresponding **`pg_combinebackup`** utility.

In addition, DBAs upgrading to PostgreSQL 17 must consider the impact of new **WAL summarization** features on their existing replication and backup strategies. With the ability to track changed blocks in the WAL, PostgreSQL 17 enables more efficient incremental backups, but this requires a shift in how WAL logs are managed. Upgrading systems with extensive replication setups will need to account for the new **failover capabilities** in logical replication, ensuring that replication slots are correctly configured to take advantage of the new features.

Furthermore, the **security enhancements**, such as the new **`pg_maintain`** role and improved event triggers for authentication, may require reconfiguring user roles and permissions to align with the new maintenance framework. DBAs will need to review their existing security policies and adjust them to ensure compatibility with the new version. For example, the new **`sslnegotiation`** parameter simplifies secure connections but may require changes in how SSL certificates are managed across the system.

The introduction of incremental backups, enhanced logical replication, performance optimizations for queries, and improved JSON handling, all together positions the PostgreSQL as a robust solution for modern data management challenges. While upgrading to PostgreSQL 17 does require thoughtful planning, the benefits it brings in terms of scalability, reliability, and flexibility make it well worth the effort for any organization.

Upgradation Strategies for PostgreSQL 17

When planning an upgrade to PostgreSQL 17 on a Linux Ubuntu system, it's essential to undertake pre-upgrade assessments and analyze potential compatibility and deprecation considerations to ensure a smooth transition. The upgrade process involves multiple layers, from the database system itself to custom configurations, extensions, and dependent applications. In the below, we will go through these preparatory steps to avoid common pitfalls and ensure your system remains stable throughout the upgrade.

Pre-Upgrade Assessments

Before proceeding with any upgrade, you must evaluate your current PostgreSQL environment to understand how the upgrade will affect your system. Pre-upgrade assessments help identify potential issues early on and allow you to mitigate risks before beginning the process.

Evaluate Current Database Version and Features

Begin by determining the current PostgreSQL version in use. Depending on how outdated your version is, there may be multiple versions between your current setup and version 17. If you are running a significantly older version (e.g., PostgreSQL 10 or earlier), you may need to account for additional changes in intermediary versions (e.g., PostgreSQL 11–16). These may include deprecations and changes in behavior that will impact your upgrade to version 17.

To check your current PostgreSQL version, use the following command in the terminal:

```
psql --version
```

Assess Hardware and System Resources

PostgreSQL 17 introduces performance improvements, but it also introduces features like enhanced parallelism, which may increase system resource utilization. Evaluate your hardware's current capacity—such as CPU, RAM, and storage—to ensure that it can handle the new requirements of PostgreSQL 17. While you do, ensure that memory-intensive features like parallel index builds and better JSON handling may consume more memory, depending on your workloads.

You may simply use **htop** and **free** to check system resources:

```
htop    # for CPU and memory usage

free -h    # for memory overview
```

If you find that system resources are constrained, you may think of scaling your infrastructure before proceeding with the upgrade.

Review Database Workloads

You need to evaluate the workloads that are currently running on your PostgreSQL instance. This includes:

- Types of queries executed (e.g., read-heavy vs. write-heavy).
- Use of features such as replication, indexing, partitioning, and foreign data wrappers.
- Use of extensions and custom configurations (e.g., stored procedures, triggers).

Workloads that rely heavily on these features might require additional testing post-upgrade. Analyze query performance using **pg_stat_statements** or run specific tests on query execution plans using the **EXPLAIN** command to understand how performance might change in version 17.

Backup the Database

While you upgrade, but never proceed to it without taking a full backup of your existing database. PostgreSQL 17 introduces changes in the storage format and metadata that are not reversible. You may use tools like **pg_basebackup** for a physical backup or **pg_dump** for a logical backup, depending on your database size and backup strategy.

For a physical backup:

```
pg_basebackup -D /path/to/backup -Fp -Xs -P
```

For a logical backup:

```
pg_dumpall > /path/to/dumpfile.sql
```

PostgreSQL 17 Compatibility Check

Review Deprecations

PostgreSQL 17 introduces a few important deprecations and changes that could impact existing systems. It's important to check your current setup for usage of deprecated features or functionality that may be removed in future versions.

- **pg_upgrade and Logical Replication:** With PostgreSQL 17, logical replication now offers better support for upgrading without dropping replication slots. However, if you are coming from an older version where this wasn't supported, you may need to update your logical replication configuration.
- **Security Settings in pg_hba.conf:** Ensure that any security settings defined in **`pg_hba.conf`** are still valid. PostgreSQL 17 introduces more refined access control features, and certain older methods or parameters may be deprecated or improved, requiring adjustments.
- **Legacy Storage Engines:** Some legacy storage options may see reduced support or performance improvements. If your system relies on older storage mechanisms, you should evaluate moving to newer options that PostgreSQL 17 optimizes for.

Check Compatibility of Extensions

PostgreSQL is known for its extensibility, and many systems use extensions to add custom functionality. Hence, you must review all extensions currently installed on your database and ensure they are compatible with version 17.

Some commonly used extensions include:

- **`pg_stat_statements`**
- **`pg_partman`** (for partition management)
- **`hstore`** and **`pg_trgm`** (for text indexing)

To check, use the **\dx** command in **psql** to list installed extensions and their versions:

```
\dx
```

Many popular extensions, such as those for partition management and text search, have been updated for better performance in version 17, but some older ones may require manual intervention during the upgrade process.

Database Drivers and Client Libraries

The PostgreSQL ecosystem includes various drivers and client libraries, such as **psycopg2** (for Python) and **pgx** (for Go). If your application relies on one of these libraries, ensure that the version you are using is fully compatible with PostgreSQL 17. Now, failing to update drivers can result in connection issues or unexpected behavior post-upgrade.

Deprecation Considerations

Configuration Deprecations

With PostgreSQL 17, some configuration parameters have either been deprecated or replaced by new ones. For example:

- **ssl_renegotiation_limit:** This setting has been deprecated. If your system uses SSL renegotiation, you will need to revise your SSL settings and adapt to the new method of handling secure connections.
- **unix_socket_directories:** If you are still using the **`unix_socket_directory`** configuration, it's been renamed to **`unix_socket_directories`** in more recent PostgreSQL versions. This change can affect environments that rely heavily on Unix domain sockets for client connections.

Check your **postgresql.conf** file for deprecated parameters and update them accordingly.

SQL Feature Deprecations

Functions that were deprecated in earlier versions (such as some old-style **`hash`** functions) may no longer be available. If your application relies on such functions, you will need to replace them with modern equivalents. Also, review your schema and application code to ensure none of your SQL queries rely on deprecated syntax or functions.

Pre-Upgrade Assessment Tools

There are several tools available to assist in pre-upgrade assessments and compatibility checks. Following are:

- **`pg_upgrade`:** A core PostgreSQL tool that helps you assess upgrade compatibility and allows for a smoother transition from one version to another.
- **`pg_dump`:** Useful for creating logical backups and testing the portability of data structures.
- **`**pgAdmin`** or **`pg_upgradecheck`:** These tools provide additional insight into potential compatibility issues, helping you address any problems before they occur.

A successful upgrade to PostgreSQL 17 can be yours if you take the time to do these pre-upgrade checks and carefully examine compatibility considerations.

Performing Upgrade

The upgrade process involves installing PostgreSQL 17 alongside the existing version, transferring data, and ensuring that custom configurations and extensions are properly handled. We will use PostgreSQL's built-in **pg_upgrade** tool for upgrading between major versions while preserving existing data.

Prepare the System

Before starting the upgrade, verify the existing PostgreSQL version and ensure that all services are running properly.

Check Current PostgreSQL Version

Run the following command to check your current PostgreSQL version (in this case, version 15):

```
psql --version
```

The output should confirm that PostgreSQL 15 is installed and active.

Install PostgreSQL 17 Packages

Add the PostgreSQL repository for version 17 to your system and install it alongside PostgreSQL 15. First, update the package lists:

```
sudo apt update
```

Then, add the PostgreSQL APT repository and install PostgreSQL 17:

```
sudo sh -c 'echo "deb
http://apt.postgresql.org/pub/repos/apt/ $(lsb_release -
cs)-pgdg main" > /etc/apt/sources.list.d/pgdg.list'

wget --quiet -O -
https://www.postgresql.org/media/keys/ACCC4CF8.asc | sudo
apt-key add -

sudo apt update
```

```
sudo apt install postgresql-17 postgresql-client-17
```

This installs PostgreSQL 17 without interfering with your PostgreSQL 15 installation.

Stop PostgreSQL Services

To safely perform the upgrade, both PostgreSQL 15 and PostgreSQL 17 services must be stopped. This prevents any write operations during the upgrade process and ensures data consistency.

```
sudo systemctl stop postgresql@15-main

sudo systemctl stop postgresql@17-main
```

Ensure that both services have stopped successfully by running:

```
sudo systemctl status postgresql
```

Prepare Data Directory

Next, wew use the **pg_upgrade** tool to handle the upgrade from PostgreSQL 15 to PostgreSQL 17. **pg_upgrade** allows you to perform in-place upgrades, where data is transferred directly from one version to another.

Backup Configuration files

Before proceeding, back up the PostgreSQL 15 configuration files (**`postgresql.conf`**, **`pg_hba.conf`**, and **`pg_ident.conf`**) to ensure you have a record of the previous settings.

```
sudo cp /etc/postgresql/15/main/*.conf /path/to/backup/
```

Run pg_upgrade Command

The **`pg_upgrade`** command requires specifying the old and new data directories and binaries. Typically, the data directories are located in **`/var/lib/postgresql/`**.

Then, run the following command to begin the upgrade process:

```
sudo -u postgres pg_upgrade \

  --old-datadir=/var/lib/postgresql/15/main \
```

```
--new-datadir=/var/lib/postgresql/17/main \
--old-bindir=/usr/lib/postgresql/15/bin \
--new-bindir=/usr/lib/postgresql/17/bin \
--link
```

After the above commands, the **`--link`** option speeds up the process by creating hard links instead of copying files, significantly reducing the time required for the upgrade, particularly for large datasets.

If any issues arise during the upgrade, **`pg_upgrade`** will provide detailed error messages. You can resolve these errors based on the specific message, such as missing files, permissions issues, or insufficient disk space.

Update Extensions

Once the upgrade completes, you must ensure that all extensions installed in PostgreSQL 15 are compatible with PostgreSQL 17. Common extensions include **pg_stat_statements**, **hstore**, and **pg_trgm**, among others. Some extensions may require upgrading their versions to work with PostgreSQL 17.

List Installed Extensions

Use the following command to list all installed extensions:

```
\dx
```

Update Extensions

For each extension, run the **`ALTER EXTENSION`** command to upgrade it to the version compatible with PostgreSQL 17. For example, to upgrade **`pg_stat_statements`**, run:

```
ALTER EXTENSION pg_stat_statements UPDATE;
```

Repeat this for all installed extensions. If an extension is not yet compatible with PostgreSQL 17, refer to the official documentation for the extension or consider disabling it until an updated version is available.

Handling Custom Extensions

If you've installed any custom or third-party extensions, verify compatibility by checking the extension's documentation. Some may need to be recompiled against the new PostgreSQL 17 libraries. You may follow this process to rebuild them:

- Download the source code for the extension.
- Recompile the extension with PostgreSQL 17's libraries.
- Install the updated extension.

Review Custom Configurations

During the upgrade, the PostgreSQL configuration files (**postgresql.conf**, **pg_hba.conf**, and **pg_ident.conf**) from version 15 are not automatically copied to the PostgreSQL 17 directory. You need to manually review and reapply custom configurations to ensure that your system continues to perform optimally.

Restore Configuration files

If you've made significant customizations to your configuration in PostgreSQL 15, copy these settings over to the PostgreSQL 17 configuration files. Start by comparing the backed-up configuration files against the default PostgreSQL 17 files.

For example, compare **`postgresql.conf`** from version 15 with the new default:

```
sudo diff /etc/postgresql/15/main/postgresql.conf
/etc/postgresql/17/main/postgresql.conf
```

Apply any custom settings from the old configuration file to the new file, ensuring compatibility with PostgreSQL 17's features and parameters.

Security Configurations (`pg_hba.conf`)

Security settings in **`pg_hba.conf`** may also need review, especially if your database handles external connections or specific authentication methods like LDAP or SSL. Ensure that all authentication mechanisms defined in PostgreSQL 15 are valid in version 17.

Open the **`pg_hba.conf`** file for PostgreSQL 17 and apply the necessary changes:

```
sudo nano /etc/postgresql/17/main/pg_hba.conf
```

Adjust New Parameters

PostgreSQL 17 introduces new configuration parameters that weren't available in previous versions. For instance, if you are using replication slots, the new **sync_replication_slots** parameter allows for synchronization of replication slots during failover, which may improve high availability setups.

If applicable, modify these settings to take advantage of PostgreSQL 17's improvements:

```
sudo nano /etc/postgresql/17/main/postgresql.conf
```

Start PostgreSQL 17

Once all configurations are in place and extensions have been updated, start the PostgreSQL 17 service:

```
sudo systemctl start postgresql@17-main
```

Verify that PostgreSQL 17 is running and that the upgraded data is intact by logging in:

```
psql -U postgres -d your_database
```

Check the PostgreSQL version again to confirm the upgrade:

```
SELECT version();
```

If everything is successful, PostgreSQL 17 should be fully operational.

Clean up Old PostgreSQL Version

After confirming that PostgreSQL 17 is running smoothly and all extensions and custom configurations are functioning as expected, you can safely remove PostgreSQL 15 to free up system resources.

Now, to remove PostgreSQL 15:

```
sudo apt remove postgresql-15

sudo rm -rf /var/lib/postgresql/15
```

With these instructions, upgrading from PostgreSQL 15 to PostgreSQL 17 will be simple, and you won't even notice a difference in how your database operates, extensions, or preferences are handled.

Post-Upgrade Validation

Now that PostgreSQL 17 has been successfully upgraded, it's important to validate that everything is functioning correctly before resuming normal operations. Now, this validation focuses on two key areas: verifying the database integrity and testing application compatibility. These steps will help confirm that your upgraded system is ready for production use as below:

Verifying Database Integrity

After an upgrade, you must first ensure that the data has been transferred correctly and that the integrity of your database is intact. Several tools and checks can be used to perform this validation.

Run pg_upgrade Validation

After completing the upgrade, run:

```
sudo -u postgres ./analyze_new_cluster.sh
```

This script is generated by **pg_upgrade** and will execute **ANALYZE** on all databases in your PostgreSQL 17 cluster. This helps the query planner collect statistics and ensures optimal query performance. It also checks for potential issues during the data migration.

Additionally, execute the following to remove the old cluster data, assuming everything is successful:

```
sudo -u postgres ./delete_old_cluster.sh
```

This command removes the old PostgreSQL 15 data directory, ensuring that there is no longer any dependency on the previous version.

Run Consistency Checks with CHECKSUMS

PostgreSQL offers the option of enabling checksums on data blocks to detect corruption. If this feature was enabled in your previous setup, you can use the following steps to ensure data consistency after the upgrade:

```
pg_verify_checksums -D /var/lib/postgresql/17/main
```

This tool checks for any data corruption in the database files, ensuring that the upgrade did not result in any loss or corruption of data.

Verify Application-Specific Data Integrity

If your PostgreSQL installation is part of a larger application, you should also perform application-specific integrity checks. This involves querying the most critical tables to ensure that no data has been altered or lost during the upgrade. You can use your application's built-in data validation tools if available, or you can run manual SQL queries to cross-check row counts and data consistency between the old and new PostgreSQL versions.

For example:

```
SELECT COUNT(*) FROM critical_table;
```

Now you compare this result to your pre-upgrade backups or logs. If you see any discrepancies in row counts or data, explore further by analyzing the logs and comparing data at a more granular level.

Analyze Database Performance

After verifying data integrity, it's essential to analyze the database's performance. PostgreSQL 17 introduces several performance enhancements, but changes in query plans and optimizations can impact performance, both positively and negatively.

Use the **EXPLAIN** and **EXPLAIN ANALYZE** commands to test the performance of key queries:

```
EXPLAIN ANALYZE SELECT * FROM large_table WHERE
condition;
```

This helps to understand whether queries are executing faster or if they require further optimization post-upgrade. If certain queries perform slower than expected, review the query plans and indexes.

Also, run **pg_stat_statements** to analyze query performance across the entire database:

```
SELECT * FROM pg_stat_statements ORDER BY total_exec_time
DESC LIMIT 10;
```

This command identifies the most time-consuming queries, allowing you to address any performance bottlenecks introduced by the upgrade.

Check Logs for Errors or Warnings

Review the logs using:

```
sudo tail -f /var/log/postgresql/postgresql-17-main.log
```

The PostgreSQL logs are an excellent source of information about potential issues following an upgrade. Pay attention to warnings or errors that appear after starting the PostgreSQL 17 server. After running the above script, look for any messages related to failed queries, slow queries, missing extensions, or security/authentication issues.

Testing Application Compatibility

Once the database integrity is confirmed, the next critical step is to ensure that your applications work seamlessly with PostgreSQL 17. This is particularly important if your application is tightly coupled with specific PostgreSQL features or behaviors that may have changed in version 17.

Test Application Connection

Many applications use client libraries, such as **libpq** for PostgreSQL, to interact with the database. These libraries must be compatible with PostgreSQL 17. To do this,

- Ensure that all application configuration files (e.g., connection strings, authentication settings) point to the upgraded PostgreSQL 17 server.
- Use application logs to check for any connection errors or warnings. If necessary, update the PostgreSQL client libraries or drivers used by your application (e.g., **psycopg2** for Python or **pgx** for Go).

Test Application Features and Queries

The next step is to test your application's functionality. This involves running all critical operations that interact with the database, such as creating, reading, updating, and deleting records. You need to pay very particular attention to any features that rely on PostgreSQL-specific features, such as stored procedures, triggers, and custom functions.

For this, review the query logs using:

```
SELECT * FROM pg_stat_activity;
```

This identifies any long-running or failed queries that could indicate compatibility issues between the application and PostgreSQL 17.

Test Extensions and Plugins

As part of your application compatibility testing, ensure that all necessary extensions are functioning correctly with PostgreSQL 17. For example, if your application uses the **pg_stat_statements** extension to monitor query performance, ensure that it's correctly installed and updated.

You can check the status of installed extensions using:

```
\dx
```

If any custom extensions were used, confirm that they are compatible with PostgreSQL 17 by testing the specific functions they provide. For example, if using **`hstore`** for key-value storage, validate that this functionality still works as expected in your application.

Test Transaction Behavior

Transaction handling is another critical area where compatibility issues may arise. PostgreSQL 17 may handle some transactions differently, particularly if new concurrency features are used.

SO, you need to ensure to test the following scenarios in your application:

- Long-running transactions
- Concurrent transactions that lock the same resources
- Complex transaction chains with rollbacks

After doing it, make sure that transaction handling works as expected and that there are no issues with deadlocks, rollbacks, or unexpected behavior.

Test Backup and Restore Procedures

Since backup and restore functionality is vital for any production system, ensure that your application's backup and restore processes work correctly with PostgreSQL 17. If your application uses **pg_dump** or **pg_basebackup** for backups, test these tools post-upgrade to confirm that they still work as expected.

For example, test a basic backup and restore with:

```
pg_dump mydb > backup.sql

pg_restore -d newdb backup.sql
```

After doing so, ensure that the restored data is complete and that no errors occur during the process.

Conduct Load Testing

Finally, conduct load testing on your application to simulate real-world usage. This helps identify potential bottlenecks or failures that may not appear during normal functional testing. There are tools like **`pgbench`** that can be used for this purpose.

For example, run a **`pgbench`** test to evaluate database performance under load:

```
pgbench -i -s 50 mydb

pgbench -c 10 -j 2 -t 10000 mydb
```

Here, you monitor system resources and query performance during load testing to ensure that PostgreSQL 17 can handle the expected workload.

All these validation steps ensure your PostgreSQL 17 upgrade is successful and that your application remains compatible and performant with the new version.

Setting up Titanic Database

Now that you have successfully upgraded to PostgreSQL 17 and validated your system, it's time to set up the Titanic sample database. The Titanic dataset will be used throughout the book for practical demonstrations of PostgreSQL features, configurations, and queries. In this section, we will walk through importing the dataset into PostgreSQL 17 and exploring its schema and data, so you become familiar with it for all the upcoming exercises.

The Titanic dataset provides valuable information about passengers aboard the RMS Titanic, including attributes like passenger class, age, gender, and whether they survived. We will first teach you through downloading and importing the **titanic.sql** file into your PostgreSQL database, then show you how to explore its schema and content.

Download Titanic Dataset

You can download the Titanic dataset from the following GitHub repository:

https://github.com/neondatabase/postgres-sample-dbs/blob/main/titanic.sql

This dataset is stored in SQL format and contains the necessary commands to recreate the Titanic table and populate it with data.

Importing Dataset into PostgreSQL

Once you've downloaded the **titanic.sql** file, follow these steps to import it into your PostgreSQL 17 instance.

Create New Database

First, create a new database where you'll store the Titanic data. Open your PostgreSQL terminal (psql) and execute the following command to create the database:

```
CREATE DATABASE titanic_db;
```

Switch to this new database:

```
\c titanic_db;
```

Import Titanic SQL file

Next, import the **titanic.sql** file into your newly created **titanic_db**. From the terminal, navigate to the directory where the **titanic.sql** file is located, and use the following command:

```
psql -U postgres -d titanic_db -f /path/to/titanic.sql
```

This command will execute all the SQL statements in the **titanic.sql** file, creating the necessary table(s) and inserting the Titanic dataset into the database.

Exploring Titanic Schema

Once the data is imported, it's essential to understand the structure (schema) of the Titanic database so you can work effectively with it throughout the book. The Titanic dataset comprises a single table named **titanic** with several columns representing different attributes of the passengers.

Inspect Table Schema

To view the schema of the **titanic** table, use the **\d** command:

```
\d titanic
```

This will display the structure of the table, showing all the columns, their data types, and any indexes or constraints. You should be able to see the following columns:

- **id**: A unique identifier for each passenger.
- **survived**: Indicates whether the passenger survived (1 = survived, 0 = did not survive).
- **pclass**: Passenger class (1st, 2nd, or 3rd class).
- **name**: The name of the passenger.
- **sex**: The gender of the passenger.
- **age**: The age of the passenger.
- **siblings_spouses_aboard**: The number of siblings or spouses aboard the Titanic with the passenger.

- **parents_children_aboard**: The number of parents or children aboard the Titanic with the passenger.
- **fare**: The fare paid by the passenger.

Check Number of Records

To get a sense of the dataset's size, check how many records (rows) are in the table:

```
SELECT COUNT(*) FROM titanic;
```

This will give you the total number of passengers recorded in the dataset, which is around 887 passengers.

View Sample Data

Now that you understand the structure, we explore the actual data. You can view a sample of the first few records using the **SELECT** command:

```
SELECT * FROM titanic LIMIT 10;
```

This command retrieves the first 10 rows of the **titanic** table, allowing you to see actual passenger data, including names, ages, fares, and whether or not they survived the disaster.

Understand Data Types and Constraints

- **Data Types**: The **survived** column uses an integer data type (1 or 0) to represent survival, while other columns like **name** use text types, and **age** and **fare** use numeric types.
- **Constraints:** This table does not have foreign keys but may include some basic constraints like NOT NULL and unique constraints on certain fields. Inspecting these will help you understand the integrity of the data.

Analyze Data Distribution

Use the following SQL queries to analyze some key characteristics of the dataset:

- Survival Rate

```
SELECT survived, COUNT(*) FROM titanic GROUP BY survived;
```

This query will show how many passengers survived versus how many did not.

- Distribution of Passenger Class

```
SELECT pclass, COUNT(*) FROM titanic GROUP BY pclass;
```

This query provides insight into the distribution of passengers across different classes (1st, 2nd, and 3rd class).

- Gender Distribution

```
SELECT sex, COUNT(*) FROM titanic GROUP BY sex;
```

This query shows the ratio of male to female passengers in the dataset.

- Age Distribution

```
SELECT age, COUNT(*) FROM titanic GROUP BY age ORDER BY
age;
```

This whole thing gives you an overview of the age distribution of the passengers, which is useful for data analysis tasks. This setup is the basis for all the practical exercises and hands-on demonstrations in the rest of the book. It'll show you exactly how to apply PostgreSQL 17's features to real-world datasets.

Summary

To summarize, we successfully upgraded PostgreSQL from version 15 to 17 and configured the Titanic sample database for future use. We started by understanding the core improvements of PostgreSQL 17 and how they affect existing systems, particularly those running Linux Ubuntu. We also looked into how the upgrade would impact extensions, custom configurations, and performance.

After laying the groundwork, we moved on to the more practical aspects of upgrading, such as preparing the system, installing PostgreSQL 17, and transferring data from PostgreSQL 15. We ensured that the old and new data directories were handled correctly and that all extensions were PostgreSQL 17 compatible. During the upgrade, we paid special attention to key extensions such as pg_stat_statements and hstore.

We had imported the Titanic dataset, familiarized ourselves with its schema and content, and were ready to go. We created a new PostgreSQL database with the titanic.sql file and examined the table structure, which included fields such as passenger class, age, fare, and survival status. We used SQL queries to analyze the dataset and gain insights into data distribution, which we will apply to future queries and optimizations.

In all, we learned all about PostgreSQL 17 and got ready to use the Titanic dataset for real-world applications in the next chapters.

CHAPTER 2: EXPERT DATABASE CLUSTER ADMINISTRATION

Brief Overview

In this chapter, we will master advanced techniques for managing PostgreSQL database clusters and gain a deeper understanding of the system's architecture. The chapter begins with an in-depth look at PostgreSQL's internal processes and memory models. You will learn how the database interacts with hardware resources and performs tasks like query execution and data management.

We will then move on to managing PostgreSQL clusters. We will focus on common administrative tasks such as starting, stopping, and monitoring clusters, especially in environments with multiple PostgreSQL instances running on a single server. This section will teach you how to control your database clusters efficiently in both development and production environments. Lastly, we will dive into advanced configuration parameters that allow you to fine-tune PostgreSQL's behavior.

Deep Dive into PostgreSQL Architecture

PostgreSQL operates using a multi-process architecture where each client connection is handled by its own process rather than a thread within a single process. This design has been consistent across many PostgreSQL versions, including PostgreSQL 17. While the architecture remains largely the same in terms of how client connections are managed, PostgreSQL 17 has introduced some optimizations that enhance performance, especially with memory management and process synchronization.

PostgreSQL 17 uses **shared memory** to store information that is required for the coordination between different backend processes. The key shared memory areas include buffer caches, transaction logs, locks, and process synchronization information. Each PostgreSQL instance allocates a fixed amount of memory during startup for shared memory, controlled by parameters like **`shared_buffers`**. Additionally, **private memory** is allocated per process for work-specific operations, with parameters such as **`work_mem`** influencing how much memory is used for sorting and other operations.

Now, compared to earlier versions, PostgreSQL 17 has introduced **parallel query enhancements** that better utilize system memory and CPU cores for complex queries, particularly those involving large datasets. The way background processes handle **shared memory** has also been fine-tuned to improve throughput in highly concurrent environments, enabling faster index builds, more efficient write-ahead logging (WAL) processing, and better query performance through parallel execution.

Background Workers

Background workers are essential processes in PostgreSQL. They perform various maintenance and auxiliary tasks. These tasks include vacuuming (removing dead tuples), writing logs to disk, handling replication, and managing autovacuum processes. Starting with PostgreSQL 9.3, users were able to define custom background workers, and this continues to be a key feature.

PostgreSQL 17 introduces improvements in background workers to handle more sophisticated tasks, including the improved handling of replication slots and memory management for background jobs. Replication slots help ensure that WAL segments needed for replication aren't prematurely removed, and PostgreSQL 17 now allows synchronization of replication slots during failovers, improving high availability setups. Autovacuum workers, responsible for cleaning up bloated tables and ensuring that indexes are maintained, also see performance improvements in environments with high data churn.

These background workers ensure that performance doesn't degrade over time, especially in databases with frequent insertions, updates, and deletions. You can also monitor and adjust the behavior of these workers through parameters in **postgresql.conf**, like **autovacuum_naptime**, **autovacuum_max_workers**, and **max_wal_senders**.

Extensions

PostgreSQL 17 continues to support a rich ecosystem of extensions, many of which have been updated to take advantage of new PostgreSQL 17 features. Some of the most common extensions include:

- **pg_stat_statements**: Provides insights into query performance by logging execution statistics.
- **hstore**: Allows key-value storage within a PostgreSQL database, providing flexibility for semi-structured data.
- **pg_trgm**: Improves full-text search capabilities by using trigram indexing, making it easier to perform fuzzy searches on text data.

The **extension management process** has been improved in this latest version to support more sophisticated use cases. For instance, logical replication slots, which are often used with replication and streaming extensions, can now be synchronized across failover scenarios, allowing for more robust high-availability deployments. This ensures that when using extensions like **pglogical** (for logical replication), you maintain a consistent and available system across multiple database instances.

Managing Database Clusters

A database cluster in PostgreSQL refers to a collection of databases that are managed by a single PostgreSQL server instance. In PostgreSQL, managing clusters includes starting, stopping, restarting services, and managing multiple clusters on the same machine. PostgreSQL allows the creation and management of multiple clusters on a single server, which is particularly useful when you need to isolate environments or run different versions of PostgreSQL simultaneously.

Here, we will practice the starting, stopping, restarting clusters, and managing multiple clusters in a PostgreSQL environment.

Starting, Stopping, and Restarting Clusters

In PostgreSQL, the management of database clusters is handled through the system's service manager, and since it is Ubuntu, this is typically **systemd**. Now, each PostgreSQL cluster has its own service, which can be managed using **systemctl**.

Starting a PostgreSQL Cluster

Starting a PostgreSQL cluster initiates the PostgreSQL server and makes the databases within that cluster accessible. To start a PostgreSQL cluster, use the following command:

```
sudo systemctl start postgresql@17-main
```

This starts the PostgreSQL 17 cluster and makes it ready for client connections. After running this command, you can check the status of the service to ensure it has started successfully:

```
sudo systemctl status postgresql@17-main
```

You should see output indicating that the cluster is running.

Stopping a PostgreSQL Cluster

Stopping a cluster gracefully shuts down the PostgreSQL server, ensuring that all open transactions are completed before closing connections. Use the following command to stop a PostgreSQL cluster:

```
sudo systemctl stop postgresql@version-main
```

For example, to stop a PostgreSQL 17 cluster:

```
sudo systemctl stop postgresql@17-main
```

Stopping a cluster prevents any new connections but allows existing transactions to complete. If you want to stop the server immediately and forcefully, you can use the **-m immediate** option:

```
sudo pg_ctlcluster 17 main stop -m immediate
```

This option is used in critical situations where the server needs to be shut down quickly, but it may result in data loss for incomplete transactions.

Restarting a PostgreSQL Cluster

Restarting a PostgreSQL cluster is necessary when you make changes to critical configuration files like **postgresql.conf** or **pg_hba.conf**. Restarting a cluster involves stopping and then immediately starting the PostgreSQL service.

To restart a PostgreSQL cluster, use the following command:

```
sudo systemctl restart postgresql@version-main
```

For example, to restart a PostgreSQL 17 cluster:

```
sudo systemctl restart postgresql@17-main
```

Restarting is necessary for applying configuration changes, but be aware that active connections to the cluster will be terminated during the restart process. Ensure that this operation is done during a maintenance window or low traffic period if you are working with a production environment.

Managing Multiple PostgreSQL Clusters

PostgreSQL allows you to manage multiple clusters on the same machine, which is useful when testing different configurations, running different versions of PostgreSQL, or isolating environments (e.g., development, staging, and production). Each cluster operates on its own port and directory, ensuring isolation between clusters.

Creating New Cluster

To create a new PostgreSQL cluster, you can use the **pg_createcluster** command. This command initializes a new cluster with its own data directory and configuration files.

For example, to create a PostgreSQL 17 cluster named **dev_cluster**:

```
sudo pg_createcluster 17 dev_cluster
```

By default, this will create a new cluster with its own data directory (typically **/var/lib/postgresql/17/dev_cluster**) and configuration files located in **/etc/postgresql/17/dev_cluster**.

Specifying Different Port for each Cluster

Each PostgreSQL cluster must run on its own port. By default, PostgreSQL listens on port 5432, but if you are running multiple clusters, you need to assign a unique port to each one. To specify a different port for the new cluster, modify the **postgresql.conf** file for the new cluster:

```
sudo nano /etc/postgresql/17/dev_cluster/postgresql.conf
```

Find the **port** setting and change it to a unique port number. For example:

```
port = 5433
```

Save the file and restart the cluster for the change to take effect:

```
sudo systemctl restart postgresql@17-dev_cluster
```

This ensures that the new cluster runs independently of any other clusters.

Managing Multiple Clusters Simultaneously

Once you have multiple clusters running, you can manage them individually using the **pg_ctlcluster** command.

To start a specific cluster, for example:

```
sudo pg_ctlcluster 17 dev_cluster start
```

To stop the same cluster:

```
sudo pg_ctlcluster 17 dev_cluster stop
```

You can also check the status of a particular cluster:

```
sudo pg_ctlcluster 17 dev_cluster status
```

This command gives you control over individual clusters, ensuring that you can manage them without disrupting other clusters running on the same machine.

Viewing and Listing Active Clusters

If you have multiple clusters running on your system and want to view all of them, you can use the **pg_lsclusters** command. This tool lists all active PostgreSQL clusters, showing their version, name, status, and port.

```
pg_lsclusters
```

The output will look something like this:

```
Ver Cluster  Port Status Owner    Data directory
Log file

17  main    5432 online postgres
/var/lib/postgresql/17/main
/var/log/postgresql/postgresql-17-main.log

17  dev_cluster 5433 online postgres
/var/lib/postgresql/17/dev_cluster
/var/log/postgresql/postgresql-17-dev_cluster.log
```

This gives you an overview of all running clusters and allows you to track which port each one is using.

Removing a Cluster

If you no longer need a specific PostgreSQL cluster, you can remove it entirely from your system. For example, to remove the **dev_cluster**:

```
sudo pg_dropcluster 17 dev_cluster
```

Be cautious when removing clusters, as this will permanently delete the data stored in that cluster.

By using tools like **pg_ctlcluster**, **pg_lsclusters**, and **systemd**, you can ensure that your PostgreSQL services run smoothly and can be easily managed across various development, testing, and production environments.

Advanced Configuration Parameters

In PostgreSQL, fine-tuning the **postgresql.conf** and **pg_hba.conf** files is essential for optimizing performance and improving security. The **postgresql.conf** file contains numerous parameters that affect database performance, including memory usage, parallelism, and query execution, while the **pg_hba.conf** file defines security-related settings such as client authentication methods and access control.

We will now demonstrate how to configure these files to ensure optimal performance and secure database access, following where we left off in managing database clusters.

Fine-Tuning `postgresql.conf`

The **postgresql.conf** file holds the primary configuration parameters for PostgreSQL and tuning this file, allows you to adjust PostgreSQL's behavior based on your system's hardware resources and workload requirements.

Below are some of the key parameters you can modify for improved performance:

Memory Allocation Settings

Efficient memory management is critical to the performance of any PostgreSQL instance, and it can be fine-tuned through parameters that control the allocation of shared memory, work memory, and caching.

- shared_buffers

This parameter defines how much memory PostgreSQL allocates for caching data pages. For most systems, this value should be set to about 25% of the total system memory.

To set it, open **`postgresql.conf`** and adjust the value:

```
sudo nano /etc/postgresql/17/main/postgresql.conf
```

Modify the **`shared_buffers`** setting:

```
shared_buffers = 4GB   # Set it to 4GB or about 25% of
total memory
```

After setting this, restart the cluster to apply changes:

```
sudo systemctl restart postgresql@17-main
```

- work_mem

This parameter controls the memory allocated for each operation (sorts, hashes, etc.) in a query. For systems running complex queries with multiple joins, this value should be higher.

Example:

```
work_mem = 64MB
```

This value is per operation, so setting it too high may cause memory issues in environments with many concurrent queries.

- maintenance_work_mem

This memory is used for maintenance tasks such as **VACUUM** and **CREATE INDEX**. Larger values improve the performance of these tasks, especially for large databases.

For example:

```
maintenance_work_mem = 1GB
```

Checkpoint Configuration

PostgreSQL writes data to disk periodically in events called **checkpoints**. These ensure data durability, but frequent checkpoints can degrade performance in write-heavy environments.

- checkpoint_completion_target

This setting controls the duration of checkpoints as a percentage of the time between checkpoints. Increasing this value spreads out writes more evenly over time, reducing the impact of checkpoints on performance.

For example:

```
checkpoint_completion_target = 0.9
```

- checkpoint_timeout

Defines how often checkpoints are triggered, with larger intervals being beneficial for reducing the frequency of I/O operations.

For example:

```
checkpoint_timeout = 15min
```

WAL Configuration

PostgreSQL uses WAL (Write-Ahead Logging) to maintain data integrity. Tuning the WAL settings can greatly improve the performance of write-heavy workloads.

- wal_buffers

This parameter controls the amount of memory used to buffer WAL data before it's written to disk. By default, PostgreSQL allocates a small value, which may not be sufficient for high-performance systems.

For example:

```
wal_buffers = 16MB
```

- max_wal_size and min_wal_size

These parameters define how much WAL data PostgreSQL keeps before triggering a checkpoint. Increasing **`max_wal_size`** can help reduce the frequency of checkpoints, improving performance during heavy write periods.

For example:

```
max_wal_size = 2GB

min_wal_size = 1GB
```

Parallelism Settings

PostgreSQL 17 has improved support for parallel query execution, which can significantly boost performance in multi-core systems. Configuring parallelism settings enables PostgreSQL to better utilize your hardware for complex queries.

- max_parallel_workers_per_gather

Defines the maximum number of workers that can be used for parallel queries. If your system has multiple CPU cores, increasing this value can improve performance for large queries.

For example:

```
max_parallel_workers_per_gather = 4
```

- max_worker_processes and max_parallel_workers

These settings control the total number of parallel worker processes PostgreSQL can spawn. Adjust these values based on your hardware and workload.

For example:

```
max_worker_processes = 8

max_parallel_workers = 8
```

Autovacuum Configuration

Autovacuum is a background process that helps maintain the health of your database by removing dead tuples and preventing table bloat. Fine-tuning autovacuum settings ensures that it runs efficiently without impacting query performance.

- autovacuum_vacuum_scale_factor

This parameter defines when autovacuum should trigger based on the number of dead tuples. Lowering this value helps prevent table bloat, especially in frequently updated tables.

For example:

```
autovacuum_vacuum_scale_factor = 0.1
```

- autovacuum_naptime

Adjusts the delay between autovacuum runs. Shorter naptimes lead to more frequent vacuuming.

For example:

```
autovacuum_naptime = 30s
```

Configuring `pg_hba.conf`

The **pg_hba.conf** (Host-Based Authentication) file controls client authentication, specifying who can connect to the database, from where, and which authentication method should be used. For maintaining a secure PostgreSQL installation, proper configuration of **pg_hba.conf** is needed.

Structure of `pg_hba.conf`

The **pg_hba.conf** file uses a simple, line-by-line configuration format with the following fields:

- **Type**: The type of connection (**`host`**, **`local`**, etc.).
- **Database**: The database(s) for which the rule applies.
- **User**: The database user(s) affected by the rule.
- **Address**: The client IP address or range that can connect.
- **Method**: The authentication method used (e.g., **`md5`**, **`scram-sha-256`**, **`peer`**).

For example, a basic rule might look like this:

```
# TYPE  DATABASE  USER  ADDRESS         METHOD

host    all       all   192.168.1.0/24  md5
```

This rule allows any user from the **192.168.1.0/24** network to connect to any database using MD5 password authentication.

Configuring IP-Based Access Control

To improve security, it's important to limit connections to trusted IP addresses or ranges. For example, to restrict access to only a specific subnet:

```
host    all         all     10.0.0.0/24     scram-sha-256
```

This rule only allows users from the **10.0.0.0/24** network to connect using the more secure **scram-sha-256** authentication method.

To allow access from localhost only (for example, for a specific database or user):

```
host    mydb        myuser  127.0.0.1/32    scram-sha-256
```

This ensures that only connections from the local machine can access **mydb** as **myuser**.

Implementing Secure Authentication Methods

PostgreSQL supports several authentication methods. While methods like **`md5`** are still widely used, it is recommended to switch to more secure options like **`scram-sha-256`**, especially for production environments.

To enforce **`scram-sha-256`** for all connections:

```
host    all         all     0.0.0.0/0       scram-sha-256
```

This requires all users connecting from any IP address to use **scram-sha-256** authentication. Additionally, you can force local connections to use more secure methods:

```
local   all         all                     peer
```

This ensures that local connections use peer authentication, which leverages the operating system's user credentials for authentication.

Restricting Superuser Access

It is a best practice to restrict superuser (e.g., **`postgres`**) access to the database. You can enforce rules in **`pg_hba.conf`** that limit access to superusers from specific trusted machines or networks.

For example, restrict the **postgres** superuser account to only allow local connections:

```
host    all         postgres   127.0.0.1/32   scram-sha-256
```

This prevents remote connections to the database using the superuser account, ensuring tighter security.

Setting up SSL Connections

For secure, encrypted connections, PostgreSQL supports SSL/TLS. To enforce SSL connections in **pg_hba.conf**, you can specify the **hostssl** type:

```
hostssl all   all   0.0.0.0/0  scram-sha-256
```

This ensures that all connections from any IP must use SSL and be authenticated with connections over a secure, encrypted channel. It ensures that all connections must be made using SSL and authenticated securely with scram-sha-256`, providing a double layer of security.

Once you have made the necessary adjustments to the **postgresql.conf** and **pg_hba.conf** files, you must restart the PostgreSQL service for the changes to take effect. You can restart the cluster with the following command:

```
sudo systemctl restart postgresql@17-main
```

Verify that the service has restarted correctly without any errors by checking the status:

```
sudo systemctl status postgresql@17-main
```

Additionally, review the PostgreSQL logs located in **/var/log/postgresql/** to ensure that the changes have been applied without any issues.

Summary

In conclusion, we demonstrated the most advanced techniques for administering PostgreSQL clusters and how to fine-tune critical configurations. We started the chapter with a detailed examination of PostgreSQL's architecture, focusing on its process and memory models. We also demonstrated the critical role of background workers in managing autovacuum, replication, and logging tasks, ensuring seamless database operations. We then moved on to the practical management of PostgreSQL clusters, learning how to start, stop, and restart clusters using system commands. Furthermore, we demonstrated how to manage multiple clusters on a single system using commands like pg_ctlcluster to control each instance individually. Each cluster can be assigned a unique port, ensuring isolation between environments.

Finally, we explored advanced configuration options by fine-tuning the postgresql.conf file to achieve optimized performance. We adjusted memory allocation settings such as shared_buffers and work_mem, configured checkpoints, and enabled parallelism for multi-core systems. We enhanced security by configuring the pg_hba.conf file, restricting access by IP address and enforcing secure authentication methods like scram-sha-256. These practices ensured that the PostgreSQL instance was both performant and secure for enterprise use.

Chapter 3: Advanced Database and Role Management

Brief Overview

In this chapter, we will master advanced techniques for managing databases and user roles in PostgreSQL. I'm going to show you how to create and manage databases using templates, schemas, and namespaces. Once you understand these concepts, you will be able to structure your databases more effectively, allowing for better organization and management of large-scale data systems.

Next, you will master Role Hierarchies and Permissions. You will learn how to define complex role structures and implement role inheritance and group roles. We will then move on to authentication mechanisms, where you will learn how to configure advanced authentication methods like LDAP, Kerberos, and SSL/TLS in PostgreSQL. Finally, we will cover fine-grained access control. You will gain an understanding of how to implement row-level security and policies for data access. This gives you precise control over which rows in a table user can view or modify, providing an additional layer of security for your database.

Sophisticated Database Management

Managing databases efficiently involves more than just creating and using them. It includes the ability to apply templates, define schemas, and organize namespaces to enhance the flexibility and scalability of your system. Here, we will recreate the Titanic database using a specific template and demonstrate how to manage schemas and namespaces effectively.

Recreating Titanic Database with a Template

A **template** in PostgreSQL is essentially a blueprint for new databases, allowing you to predefine certain structures, tables, or settings that you want to carry over to new databases. PostgreSQL comes with two built-in templates by default: **template0** and **template1**. While **template1** is often used as a base, we can create custom templates for specific use cases.

In this demonstration, we will recreate the Titanic database, but we will first explore how to create and use a different template.

Create a Custom Template Database

First, we create a custom template database. This could be a database with some pre-defined settings or objects that we want to reuse for future databases.

- Connect to PostgreSQL using **`psql`**:

```
psql -U postgres
```

- Create a new database named **`template_titanic`** as a custom template:

```
CREATE DATABASE template_titanic;
```

- Make sure to mark this database as a template by altering its properties:

```
UPDATE pg_database SET datistemplate = TRUE WHERE datname
= 'template_titanic';
```

We can now add any specific configurations, extensions, or objects to this database that we want future databases to inherit. For instance, we can add some predefined settings, tables, or even extensions like **`pg_stat_statements`**.

After setting up, we revoke all connect privileges to avoid any direct connections to this template:

```
REVOKE CONNECT ON DATABASE template_titanic FROM PUBLIC;
```

Recreate Titanic Database using a Template

Now that we have our custom template, we can use it to create our Titanic database. The new database will inherit the schema and objects from **template_titanic**.

- Drop the existing Titanic database (if needed):

```
DROP DATABASE IF EXISTS titanic_db;
```

- Recreate the Titanic database using **`template_titanic`**:

```
CREATE DATABASE titanic_db TEMPLATE template_titanic;
```

At this point, the **titanic_db** is an exact copy of the **template_titanic** database, including any predefined settings or objects you might have added. You can now proceed to load the Titanic dataset or modify the new database further.

Managing Schemas and Namespaces

Schemas provide a way to logically separate and organize database objects such as tables, views, and functions within a database. This allows for greater flexibility in managing complex systems where multiple teams or applications may share a single database, but need distinct object spaces.

A **namespace** in PostgreSQL is effectively the same as a schema; it's a logical container for database objects. Multiple schemas can coexist within a single database, allowing you to separate different types of data or users without creating separate databases.

Understanding Default Schema Behavior

By default, PostgreSQL databases come with a schema called **public**, where all tables and objects are placed if no other schema is specified. However, as the database grows or you have multiple users or applications, you may want to organize objects into different schemas.

We will explore the current schema setup in the Titanic database as follows:

- First, switch to the Titanic database:

```
\c titanic_db
```

- List the current schemas in the database:

```
\dn
```

You should see the default **public** schema listed.

Create and use Custom Schemas

Next, we create a custom schema to organize our tables and other objects more effectively. For example, we can create a schema specifically for Titanic-related data.

- Create a schema called **`titanic_data`**:

```
CREATE SCHEMA titanic_data;
```

- Create a new table in the **`titanic_data`** schema instead of the default **`public`** schema:

```
CREATE TABLE titanic_data.passengers (

    id SERIAL PRIMARY KEY,

    name VARCHAR(100),

    age INT,

    gender VARCHAR(10),
```

```
    survived BOOLEAN
);
```

This creates the **passengers** table within the **titanic_data** schema, instead of the **public** schema.

Switching between Schemas

By default, PostgreSQL looks for tables and objects in the **public** schema unless otherwise specified. If you have multiple schemas in your database, you can change the search path to control which schema PostgreSQL searches first.

- To list the current search path:

```
SHOW search_path;
```

By default, the search path will include the **public** schema.

- You can modify the search path to prioritize the **`titanic_data`** schema:

```
SET search_path TO titanic_data, public;
```

Now, when you run queries without specifying a schema, PostgreSQL will first search in **titanic_data** and then in **public**.

For example:

```
SELECT * FROM passengers;
```

This query will now refer to the **passengers** table in the **titanic_data** schema since it's prioritized in the search path.

Managing Object Access between Schemas

Schemas can also be used to manage access control between different database objects. For example, you might want to allow certain users to read from a schema but restrict them from writing to it.

- Create a new role or user:

```
CREATE USER titanic_user WITH PASSWORD 'password123';
```

- Grant **SELECT** permission on the **titanic_data** schema to the new user:

```
GRANT USAGE ON SCHEMA titanic_data TO titanic_user;

GRANT SELECT ON ALL TABLES IN SCHEMA titanic_data TO
titanic_user;
```

This ensures that the **titanic_user** can read from the tables in the **titanic_data** schema but cannot modify or create new objects within that schema.

- If needed, you can grant additional permissions, such as allowing the user to create new tables in the schema:

```
GRANT CREATE ON SCHEMA titanic_data TO titanic_user;
```

Moving Objects between Schemas

Sometimes you might want to move tables or other objects between schemas, particularly if you are reorganizing your database.

For example, to move the **passengers** table from the **titanic_data** schema to the **public** schema:

```
ALTER TABLE titanic_data.passengers SET SCHEMA public;
```

This command moves the **passengers** table from the **titanic_data** schema back to the **public** schema. Moving objects between schemas helps in cases where you want to reorganize objects or adjust how different schemas are utilized.

Dropping Schemas

If a schema is no longer needed, you can drop it. Be cautious, as this will remove all objects within the schema.

To drop the **titanic_data** schema:

```
DROP SCHEMA titanic_data CASCADE;
```

The **CASCADE** option ensures that all objects within the schema are also dropped. If you want to drop the schema but retain the objects, you must first move them to another schema using **ALTER TABLE**.

With the help of schemas and namespaces, objects can be logically separated, which improves database organization, control of access, and design flexibility. As you work with PostgreSQL in various use cases, this knowledge will help you handle more complex database environments.

Role Hierarchies and Permissions

The management of user roles and permissions can become complex, especially in environments where multiple users or applications require varying degrees of access to different parts of the database. PostgreSQL's role-based access control system allows you to create **role hierarchies**, define **group roles**, and implement **role inheritance** to simplify user management and security.

Using the Titanic database, we will learn to practically define the complex role structures, set up role inheritance, and manage permissions.

Sample Program: Role Hierarchies and Permissions

Consider the following scenario for managing access in the Titanic database:

1. You have a **data engineering team** responsible for loading, transforming, and updating data in the **`titanic_data`** schema.
2. A **data analyst team** needs read-only access to the tables in the **`titanic_data`** schema for generating reports and querying data.
3. An **admin role** must oversee all operations, including managing roles, creating schemas, and executing privileged operations.

In this situation, the goal is to:

- Define complex role hierarchies with appropriate permissions for each group.
- Implement role inheritance so that members of each team automatically inherit the correct permissions.
- Create group roles to simplify user management and ensure that permissions are granted efficiently.

Defining Basic Roles

First, we will create basic roles for each user group: the data engineers, data analysts, and administrators. To begin, create individual roles for the **data engineers** and **data analysts**. These roles will not be directly assigned to users yet but will be used to define permissions:

```
CREATE ROLE data_engineer NOLOGIN;

CREATE ROLE data_analyst NOLOGIN;
```

The **NOLOGIN** attribute means these roles are not used directly by users for login but serve as group roles that other roles can inherit permissions from. This simplifies permission management when dealing with multiple users.

Creating Admin Role

Next, create the **admin role**, which will have more advanced privileges:

```
CREATE ROLE titanic_admin WITH LOGIN PASSWORD
'admin_password';
```

This role is assigned the **LOGIN** privilege, meaning it can be used by the administrator to log into the database and manage users, roles, and permissions.

Now that we have created the roles, we need to assign permissions that match their responsibilities. In PostgreSQL, we can grant permissions on specific database objects such as schemas, tables, and sequences. These permissions include **SELECT**, **INSERT**, **UPDATE**, **DELETE**, and **USAGE** (on schemas), among others.

Granting Permissions to Data Engineering Role

The **data engineering team** requires full access to the **titanic_data** schema, including the ability to insert, update, delete, and select data. We will grant those permissions:

```
GRANT USAGE ON SCHEMA titanic_data TO data_engineer;

GRANT SELECT, INSERT, UPDATE, DELETE ON ALL TABLES IN
SCHEMA titanic_data TO data_engineer;
```

The **USAGE** privilege allows the **data_engineer** role to access the schema, while the other privileges (**SELECT**, **INSERT**, **UPDATE**, and **DELETE**) give full control over the tables within the **titanic_data** schema.

Granting Read-Only Permissions to Data Analyst Role

The **data analysts** need read-only access to the same schema, meaning they should only be able to run **SELECT** queries to retrieve data. Grant them read-only access:

```
GRANT USAGE ON SCHEMA titanic_data TO data_analyst;

GRANT SELECT ON ALL TABLES IN SCHEMA titanic_data TO
data_analyst;
```

This setup ensures that the **data_analyst** role can only read data without modifying it.

Granting Elevated Permissions to Admin Role

The **admin role** will oversee both teams and have higher privileges to manage the entire database, including the ability to create schemas, manage roles, and perform administrative tasks.

```
GRANT ALL PRIVILEGES ON SCHEMA titanic_data TO
titanic_admin;

GRANT CREATE ON DATABASE titanic_db TO titanic_admin;

GRANT ROLE data_engineer TO titanic_admin;

GRANT ROLE data_analyst TO titanic_admin;
```

This grants the **titanic_admin** role full privileges on the **titanic_data** schema and allows the administrator to create new objects in the **titanic_db** database. The administrator can also inherit permissions from both **data_engineer** and **data_analyst**, giving them full control over all database operations.

Role Inheritance and Group Roles

Roles can **inherit** permissions from other roles. This feature builds **role hierarchies**, where higher-level roles automatically inherit the privileges of lower-level roles. We will implement role inheritance so that individual team members inherit permissions from their respective group roles.

Creating Group Roles for each Team

Group roles serve as a way to manage multiple users within a team without assigning permissions to each user individually. Create group roles for the data engineers and data analysts:

```
CREATE ROLE engineering_team INHERIT;

CREATE ROLE analyst_team INHERIT;
```

The **INHERIT** attribute means that users assigned to these group roles will automatically inherit the permissions of the roles they are associated with.

Assigning Group Roles to Team Members

Next, assign specific users to the newly created group roles. Assume we have two users: **alice** for the data engineers and **bob** for the data analysts. For this, create the individual user roles:

```
CREATE USER alice WITH PASSWORD 'password123';

CREATE USER bob WITH PASSWORD 'password123';
```

Assign these users to their respective group roles:

```
GRANT engineering_team TO alice;

GRANT analyst_team TO bob;
```

Assigning Role Inheritance to Group Roles

Now, we can make the **group roles** inherit the privileges of the **data_engineer** and **data_analyst** roles:

```
GRANT data_engineer TO engineering_team;

GRANT data_analyst TO analyst_team;
```

With this setup, all users assigned to **engineering_team** inherit the privileges of the **data_engineer** role, and users in **analyst_team** inherit the privileges of the **data_analyst** role.

Testing Role Inheritance

You can now test the role inheritance by logging in as **alice** and **bob** and running some queries:

- Log in as Alice:

```
psql -U alice -d titanic_db
```

- Verify Alice's permissions by running an **INSERT** query:

```
INSERT INTO titanic_data.passengers (name, age, gender,
survived) VALUES ('Alice Doe', 30, 'female', true);
```

Alice should be able to insert data into the table, as she inherits the **data_engineer** role's permissions. Now, do testing for Bob (data analyst):

- Log in as Bob:

```
psql -U bob -d titanic_db
```

- Verify Bob's permissions by running a **SELECT** query:

```
SELECT * FROM titanic_data.passengers;
```

Bob should be able to query the data but not insert, update, or delete records, as he inherits the read-only **data_analyst** role.

Managing Role Privileges and Revoking Permissions

With the database growing, you may need to adjust or revoke permissions from specific users or roles. For example, if Alice moves to a different team and no longer needs access to the Titanic database, you can revoke her privileges:

```
REVOKE engineering_team FROM alice;
```

This immediately removes Alice from the **engineering_team** group, and she will no longer inherit the permissions of the **data_engineer** role.

If needed, you can also revoke specific privileges from a role. For instance, to prevent the **data_analyst** role from selecting from certain tables:

```
REVOKE SELECT ON titanic_data.passengers FROM
data_analyst;
```

With this, we have seen how to define complex role hierarchies and manage permissions in PostgreSQL, using the Titanic database as an example. We created distinct roles for data engineers, data analysts, and administrators, assigned appropriate permissions, and implemented role inheritance through group roles. This structure simplifies user management and ensures that permissions are granted efficiently, while still allowing for flexibility and control over who can access and modify data in the database.

Authentication Mechanisms

We will configure **pg_hba.conf** to further control who can access the Titanic database from remote hosts. We will set up rules for remote connections, allowing access only from specific IP ranges and securing the connection with a strong authentication method.

Restrict Remote Access by IP Range

If your database allows remote access, it's important to restrict the IP addresses that can connect. For example, if only users on the internal network **192.168.1.0/24** are allowed to connect to **titanic_db**, you can add the following line to **pg_hba.conf**:

```
host    titanic_db    all    192.168.1.0/24    scram-sha-
256
```

This rule allows any user from the internal network to connect to the Titanic database using **scram-sha-256** authentication, ensuring that all communications are secure.

Restricting Superuser Access

To enhance security, it's a good idea to restrict remote access for superuser roles like **postgres**. You can restrict this account to local connections only, preventing remote logins:

```
host    all    postgres    0.0.0.0/0    reject
```

This rule explicitly rejects any remote connection attempts from the **postgres** superuser role, ensuring that this critical account is protected from unauthorized access.

Integrating LDAP

LDAP (Lightweight Directory Access Protocol) is commonly used in organizations for centralized authentication. PostgreSQL supports LDAP integration, allowing database users to authenticate against an LDAP server.

Now, to enable LDAP-based authentication, you need to modify the **`pg_hba.conf`** file to include an **`ldap`** rule. For instance, we configure PostgreSQL to authenticate Titanic database users via LDAP.

For this, in **`pg_hba.conf`**, add the following:

```
host    titanic_db    all    192.168.1.0/24    ldap
ldapserver=ldap.gitforgits.com
ldapbinddn="cn=admin,dc=gitforgits,dc=com"
ldapbindpasswd=admin_password ldapsearchattribute=uid
ldapbasedn="dc=gitforgits,dc=com"
```

This rule allows users from the IP range **192.168.1.0/24** to authenticate using their LDAP credentials. The key components here include:

- **ldapserver**: The hostname or IP of your LDAP server.
- **ldapbinddn**: The distinguished name (DN) used to bind to the LDAP server.
- **ldapbasedn**: The base DN to search for users in the LDAP directory.

Once the LDAP rule is in place, ensure that the users who need access to the Titanic database have accounts in the LDAP directory. PostgreSQL will authenticate these users by checking their credentials against the LDAP server.

Integrating Kerberos Authentication

Kerberos is a network authentication protocol that uses tickets to allow secure authentication over an insecure network. PostgreSQL supports Kerberos integration for environments where Kerberos is the preferred method of authentication.

Configuring Kerberos in 'pg_hba.conf'

Now, to configure Kerberos authentication, you need to install and configure a Kerberos server and ensure that PostgreSQL is configured to use Kerberos tickets for authentication. In **pg_hba.conf**, add a rule like the following:

```
host    titanic_db    all    192.168.1.0/24    gss
include_realm=1 krb_realm=EXAMPLE.COM
```

Here,

- **gss**: Specifies the use of Kerberos authentication.
- **krb_realm**: The Kerberos realm your PostgreSQL server is part of (e.g., **EXAMPLE.COM**).
- **include_realm**: Determines whether the full Kerberos realm is included in the authentication check.

Setting up PostgreSQL Server

Ensure that your PostgreSQL server is properly integrated with the Kerberos infrastructure by configuring **krb_server_keyfile** in **postgresql.conf**:

```
krb_server_keyfile = '/etc/postgresql/krb5.keytab'
```

This keytab file stores the service principal and key that PostgreSQL will use to authenticate with the Kerberos server.

Verifying Kerberos Authentication

Once Kerberos is configured, users can authenticate using their Kerberos tickets. For instance, a user can request a Kerberos ticket with:

```
kinit username
```

Then they can connect to the PostgreSQL database without needing to provide a password, as the ticket is used for authentication.

Enabling SSL/TLS

Here, securing the connections between PostgreSQL and clients over the network is essential, especially when sensitive data is being transmitted. PostgreSQL supports SSL/TLS to encrypt traffic and protect data in transit.

Configuring SSL

To enable SSL, you need to configure PostgreSQL to use a certificate and private key. In **postgresql.conf**, enable SSL and specify the certificate and key locations:

```
ssl = on

ssl_cert_file = '/etc/postgresql/ssl/server.crt'

ssl_key_file = '/etc/postgresql/ssl/server.key'
```

Make sure the certificate and key files are properly generated and installed. The key file should only be readable by the PostgreSQL user for security reasons:

```
chmod 600 /etc/postgresql/ssl/server.key
```

Configuring 'pg_hba.conf' for SSL

To enforce SSL connections in **pg_hba.conf**, add a rule that requires SSL for all connections. You can use the **hostssl** type to enforce SSL:

```
hostssl    titanic_db    all    0.0.0.0/0    scram-sha-
256
```

This ensures that all connections to the Titanic database are encrypted using SSL and authenticated using **scram-sha-256**.

Enforcing Client Certificates

For additional security, you can enforce client certificates for SSL connections. This requires that clients present a valid certificate when connecting to the PostgreSQL server. In **postgresql.conf**, add:

```
ssl_ca_file = '/etc/postgresql/ssl/ca.crt'

ssl_crl_file = '/etc/postgresql/ssl/crl.pem'
```

This ensures that only clients with certificates signed by your CA can connect to PostgreSQL. You also need to adjust **pg_hba.conf** to require client certificates:

```
hostssl    titanic_db    all    0.0.0.0/0    cert
clientcert=1
```

With this rule, only clients with valid certificates can establish a connection.

Testing SSL Connections

Once SSL is configured, you can verify that clients are connecting securely by checking the PostgreSQL logs and using the **psql** command-line tool:

```
psql "sslmode=require host=your_postgresql_server
dbname=titanic_db user=titanic_user"
```

By integrating advanced authentication mechanisms like LDAP, Kerberos, and SSL/TLS, you can secure access to your PostgreSQL databases while maintaining flexibility in user management.

Fine-Grained Access Control

Fine-grained access control allows you to control who can view or modify specific data at a row level rather than just at a table level. PostgreSQL offers **Row-Level Security (RLS)**, which lets you define policies to restrict access to rows in a table based on specific conditions. This is particularly useful when different users require access to subsets of data within the same table. Continuing from where we left off in the previous section, we will now implement row-level security and data access policies for the Titanic database.

Enabling Row-Level Security (RLS)

Row-level security ensures that access to rows in a table is restricted based on defined conditions. First, we need to enable RLS on a table before defining policies. Here, we will start by enabling RLS on the **passengers** table in the **titanic_data** schema.

- First, connect to the Titanic database as an admin:

```
\c titanic_db
```

- Enable row-level security for the **`passengers`** table:

```
ALTER TABLE titanic_data.passengers ENABLE ROW LEVEL
SECURITY;
```

With RLS enabled, no row-level policies are applied yet. Without explicit policies, users can still access all rows in the table. Now, we will define policies to control access based on specific conditions.

Implementing Row-Level Security Policies

RLS policies determine who can access or modify which rows based on conditions you define. In our case, we will define two policies:

- Data engineers (with the **`data_engineer`** role) can view and modify all passenger data.
- Data analysts (with the **`data_analyst`** role) can only view rows where the passenger's age is above 18 (adult passengers).

Define a Policy for Data Engineers

Data engineers require full access to all rows in the **passengers** table. We can define a policy that allows them to select, insert, update, or delete any rows.

Create the policy for data engineers:

```
CREATE POLICY engineer_full_access ON
titanic_data.passengers

FOR ALL

USING (true)
```

```
WITH CHECK (true)

TO data_engineer;
```

In the above, the **USING** clause defines a condition that must be met for a user to access rows. In this case, we set it to **true**, allowing access to all rows for users in the **data_engineer** role. Similarly, the **WITH CHECK** clause ensures that engineers can modify all rows as well.

Define a Policy for Data Analysts

Data analysts should have read-only access, and they should only see rows where the passenger is over 18 years old. We will define a policy that restricts their access to these rows.

Create the policy for data analysts:

```
CREATE POLICY analyst_read_access ON
titanic_data.passengers

FOR SELECT

USING (age > 18)

TO data_analyst;
```

In this policy, the **USING** clause restricts access to rows where the age is greater than 18. This allows analysts to view only adult passengers, and it applies only to **SELECT** queries (no modification privileges are granted).

Testing Row-Level Security Policies

Now that we have implemented row-level security policies for data engineers and data analysts, we test these policies to ensure they work as expected.

Testing for Data Engineers

Log in as a user with the **data_engineer** role (e.g., **alice**).

- Connect to the Titanic database as Alice:

```
psql -U alice -d titanic_db
```

- Run a query to select all rows from the **passengers** table:

```
SELECT * FROM titanic_data.passengers;
```

Since Alice is part of the **data_engineer** role, she should be able to see all rows in the table.

- Test data modification by inserting a new row:

```
INSERT INTO titanic_data.passengers (name, age, gender,
survived) VALUES ('John Doe', 35, 'male', true);
```

This insertion should be successful since the policy allows data engineers full access to the table.

Testing for Data Analysts

Now log in as a user with the **data_analyst** role (e.g., **bob**).

- Connect to the Titanic database as Bob:

```
psql -U bob -d titanic_db
```

- Run a query to select all rows from the **passengers** table:

```
SELECT * FROM titanic_data.passengers;
```

Bob should only see rows where the **age** is greater than 18, as per the policy we defined.

- Test data modification by attempting to insert a row:

```
INSERT INTO titanic_data.passengers (name, age, gender,
survived) VALUES ('Jane Doe', 22, 'female', false);
```

This query should fail because Bob does not have **INSERT** privileges. The policy restricts him to read-only access, and only for rows where **age > 18**.

Restricting Access Based on User Identity

Row-level security policies can also be customized to meet various use cases. We will implement a few more scenarios to demonstrate how flexible RLS can be in PostgreSQL. If you want to restrict access based on the logged-in user, PostgreSQL provides a special variable called **current_user** that holds the name of the user currently connected to the database. We will assume we want to restrict analysts so they can only view the data they've entered.

- First, alter the **passengers** table to include an **entered_by** column to track the user who inserted each row:

```
ALTER TABLE titanic_data.passengers ADD COLUMN entered_by
VARCHAR(100);
```

- Create a new policy that allows analysts to view only the rows they've inserted:

```
CREATE POLICY analyst_own_data ON titanic_data.passengers

FOR SELECT

USING (entered_by = current_user)

TO data_analyst;
```

This policy restricts analysts to only viewing the rows where the **entered_by** column matches their username.

- Insert a row as an analyst (e.g., **bob**):

```
INSERT INTO titanic_data.passengers (name, age, gender,
survived, entered_by) VALUES ('Mark Smith', 29, 'male',
true, current_user);
```

Now, Bob will only be able to see the rows he has inserted, and not rows entered by other users.

Combining Multiple Policies

PostgreSQL allows you to combine multiple row-level security policies on the same table. For instance, you can define one policy that restricts data analysts to seeing only their own data, and another that restricts them to seeing only rows where the passenger is over 18.

```
CREATE POLICY analyst_age_limit ON
titanic_data.passengers

FOR SELECT

USING (age > 18)
```

```
TO data_analyst;
```

With both the **analyst_own_data** and **analyst_age_limit** policies in place, analysts will only be able to see rows where the passenger's age is over 18 **and** they entered the data themselves.

Managing Row-Level Security and Policies

You can manage your row-level security policies by listing, altering, or dropping them as needed.

To do this, first list all policies on a table:

```
\d+ titanic_data.passengers
```

This command will display all policies applied to the **passengers** table. If you want to modify a policy, you can use the **ALTER POLICY** command. For example, to change the condition for the **analyst_age_limit** policy:

```
ALTER POLICY analyst_age_limit ON titanic_data.passengers
USING (age >= 21);
```

And, to remove a policy, use the **DROP POLICY** command. For example, to drop the **analyst_own_data** policy:

```
DROP POLICY analyst_own_data ON titanic_data.passengers;
```

This level of access control is crucial for environments where users have varying permissions or need restricted views of the data. The flexibility of PostgreSQL's RLS system allows you to tailor data access policies to meet a wide range of use cases, ensuring security and proper data governance across your database systems.

Summary

To sum up, we focused on advanced database and role management. We got to grips with recreating the Titanic database using templates and organizing data with schemas and namespaces. Next, we explored the concept of role hierarchies and permissions. We created roles for different teams, such as data engineers and data analysts, and assigned them varying levels of access to the Titanic database. We showed how to use role inheritance and group roles to make managing permissions much more efficient.

We then moved on to authentication mechanisms, configuring advanced settings in the pg_hba.conf file and integrating PostgreSQL with external authentication services like LDAP, Kerberos, and SSL/TLS. Finally, we implemented fine-grained access control using row-level security (RLS). This chapter provided a comprehensive understanding of how to manage roles, permissions, and security at a granular level in PostgreSQL.

CHAPTER 4: CONFIGURATION AND PERFORMANCE TUNING

Brief Overview

This chapter will focus on advanced PostgreSQL configuration and tuning techniques for achieving optimal performance in various environments. We'll start with Optimizing Server Performance, where you'll learn to fine-tune PostgreSQL's core settings to make the most of your system's hardware resources. This includes adjusting memory settings, parallelism, and query performance parameters that directly impact how the server handles large workloads.

Next, we will examine how PostgreSQL creates and executes query plans in depth. You will learn how to use EXPLAIN and EXPLAIN ANALYZE to understand query performance and make necessary optimizations. You can improve execution times by understanding how the PostgreSQL optimizer works and rewriting or adjusting queries as needed. You will also learn how to manage system resources, including CPU and memory, effectively. We will examine connection pooling with tools like pgBouncer, handle high workloads with pg_stat_statements, and configure settings like work_mem to optimize for different types of operations.

Finally, you will learn how to configure PostgreSQL's logging settings to capture important performance and security data. This will include setting up detailed logs for query performance analysis and configuring auditing with pgaudit to monitor and track database activities for security and compliance. This is the chapter that will equip you with the skills needed to fine-tune and monitor your PostgreSQL instance effectively.

Optimizing Server Performance

So far, we have learned how to create and manage our Titanic database in PostgreSQL, from setting up user roles and permissions to applying fine-grained access controls through row-level security (RLS). We've also explored authentication mechanisms and integrated our database with external authentication systems like LDAP, Kerberos, and SSL/TLS. Now, we shift our focus to ensuring that our PostgreSQL instance is running at its peak performance by fine-tuning server settings. Understanding how to optimize memory usage, configure key parameters, and manage system resources is essential for maintaining a database that handles heavy workloads efficiently.

Memory and Resource Allocation Strategies

In PostgreSQL, resource allocation, particularly memory impacts server performance. The database engine uses a combination of **shared memory** and **local memory** to handle everything from query execution to caching, which determines how fast queries are processed and how effectively the database can serve concurrent users. Poorly allocated memory can result in slow query performance, excessive disk I/O, and bottlenecks in throughput.

Key memory-related parameters that affect PostgreSQL performance include **`shared_buffers`**, **`work_mem`**, and **`maintenance_work_mem`**. These settings allow us to allocate system memory effectively, ensuring that queries run faster and overall performance is optimized.

Configuring Database Caching

The **shared_buffers** parameter defines the amount of memory PostgreSQL allocates for caching data pages in memory. This memory is shared among all the database connections and acts as a buffer between the database and disk I/O. Configuring **shared_buffers** correctly is crucial because the more data that can be cached in memory, the less PostgreSQL has to retrieve from disk, leading to faster query execution.

For most production environments, a common recommendation is to set **shared_buffers** to 25% of your system's total memory. However, depending on the workload and the amount of available RAM, this value may be increased. Below, we will configure **shared_buffers** for our PostgreSQL instance:

- Open the **postgresql.conf** file:

```
sudo nano /etc/postgresql/17/main/postgresql.conf
```

- Locate the **shared_buffers** setting and set it to 25% of your system's total RAM. For example, if your system has 16GB of RAM, you can set:

```
shared_buffers = 4GB
```

- Save the file and restart PostgreSQL for the changes to take effect:

```
sudo systemctl restart postgresql@17-main
```

This configuration allocates 4GB of memory for shared buffers, which helps PostgreSQL reduce disk access by keeping more data in memory.

Memory Allocation for Operations

The **work_mem** setting controls the amount of memory allocated to each individual operation, such as sorts, hash joins, and aggregations. Here, note that **work_mem** is allocated per operation per query, meaning that a high **work_mem** value can lead to excessive memory usage when multiple operations are executed concurrently. Nw, to configure **work_mem**, you need to balance the trade-off between memory usage and performance. For environments where complex queries with large sorts and joins are common, increasing **work_mem** can speed up query execution.

Following is the example of how to configure **work_mem**:

- Open **postgresql.conf,** and locate the **work_mem** setting. For systems handling complex queries but with a moderate number of concurrent users, a good starting point might be 64MB:

```
work_mem = 64MB
```

This setting provides each operation with 64MB of memory, which improves performance for sorts and joins without using too much system memory.

Memory for Maintenance Tasks

The **maintenance_work_mem** setting is used for maintenance operations such as **VACUUM**, **CREATE INDEX**, and **ALTER TABLE**. By default, PostgreSQL sets **maintenance_work_mem** to a relatively low value, which may not be sufficient for databases with large tables or heavy data insertion workloads. For production environments, you can configure **maintenance_work_mem** to around 10-20% of total memory to ensure that maintenance operations are efficient.

To configure **maintenance_work_mem**, open the **postgresql.conf**, and set the **maintenance_work_mem** to a higher value, such as 2GB, for larger databases:

```
maintenance_work_mem = 2GB
```

With this setting, PostgreSQL can use up to 2GB of memory for maintenance tasks, allowing it to handle larger tables and complex maintenance operations more efficiently.

Estimating Available Memory

While **shared_buffers** controls the memory allocated for caching within PostgreSQL, the **effective_cache_size** parameter tells PostgreSQL how much of the system's memory is available for disk caching by the operating system. This parameter doesn't allocate memory directly, but it helps PostgreSQL's query planner estimate the amount of memory available for caching data and making decisions on whether to use indexes.

A common recommendation for **effective_cache_size** is to set it to 50-75% of the system's total RAM, which reflects the portion of the system memory that the OS will likely use for disk cache. To do this, open **postgresql.conf**, and set the value of **effective_cache_size**. For a system with 16GB of RAM, setting it to 12GB would be appropriate:

```
effective_cache_size = 12GB
```

This configuration helps PostgreSQL's query planner make better decisions, especially when choosing between sequential scans and index scans.

Other Key Parameters for Optimizing Performance

Beyond memory allocation, there are several other key parameters that can significantly impact PostgreSQL performance, especially in high-traffic or resource-constrained environments.

Limiting Concurrent Connections

The **max_connections** parameter controls the maximum number of concurrent connections that can be made to the PostgreSQL instance. By default, this value is set to 100, but in busy environments, you may want to adjust this value to better suit your hardware resources.

If too many connections are allowed, each connection consumes memory, which can lead to performance degradation. However, setting the value too low can limit the system's ability to handle multiple users.

To adjust **max_connections**, add the following in **`postgresql.conf`**:

```
max_connections = 300
```

Increasing the number of connections will allow more users to interact with the database simultaneously, but it must be configured in conjunction with memory allocation to prevent overuse of resources.

Adjusting Checkpoint Frequency

The **checkpoint_completion_target** parameter controls the rate at which PostgreSQL writes these changes to disk, expressed as a percentage of the time between checkpoints. A higher value spreads the I/O more evenly and reduces performance spikes caused by checkpoints.

To do this, set the **`checkpoint_completion_target`** in **`postgresql.conf`**:

```
checkpoint_completion_target = 0.9
```

This setting instructs PostgreSQL to aim for completing 90% of the checkpoint work in the available time, reducing the impact of sudden disk I/O spikes.

Tuning Write-Ahead Logging

The **`wal_buffers`** parameter controls the amount of memory allocated for buffering write-ahead log entries before they are flushed to disk. Increasing this value is particularly helpful for write-heavy environments where many transactions are being committed. The default value is often too low for larger databases.

To configure **wal_buffers**, add the following in **postgresql.conf**:

```
wal_buffers = 16MB
```

This setting allows PostgreSQL to handle a higher volume of transactions before writing them to disk, reducing write overhead during busy periods.

By optimizing memory and resource allocation, we ensure that the server performs is at its best, thereby reducing latency and maximizing the throughput. These adjustments are good tunings for managing both routine operations and complex queries in a production environment.

Query Planning and Execution

PostgreSQL's **query optimizer** is a key component of the database system that determines the most efficient way to execute a query. The optimizer evaluates multiple possible execution plans and selects the one with the lowest estimated cost. These costs are influenced by various factors, such as the size of the tables, indexes, and statistics. The query planner evaluates factors like joins, sorting, and filtering to estimate the most efficient path for executing queries, making sure the database performs optimally.

In this section, we will take a practical approach to understanding how PostgreSQL's query planner works using two essential tools: **EXPLAIN** and **EXPLAIN ANALYZE**. These tools help you visualize and analyze query execution plans, giving you insights into how your queries are executed, what resources are being used, and where optimizations can be made.

Using **EXPLAIN** to understand Query Plans

The **EXPLAIN** command provides a high-level overview of the execution plan that PostgreSQL intends to follow for a given query. This execution plan includes details about how data will be fetched, what indexes (if any) will be used, and the estimated costs associated with each operation.

We will teach to make use **EXPLAIN** on a sample query for the Titanic database, lets say for example, we want to fetch all passengers from the **passengers** table who survived.

```
EXPLAIN SELECT * FROM titanic_data.passengers WHERE
survived = true;
```

The result will look something like this:

```
Seq Scan on titanic_data.passengers  (cost=0.00..25.30
rows=120 width=70)
```

```
  Filter: (survived = true)
```

Here,

- **Seq Scan** means PostgreSQL is performing a sequential scan of the entire **passengers** table. This is often used when no indexes are available for the query.
- The two numbers (**0.00..25.30**) represent the estimated start-up cost and total cost for fetching the rows.
- The optimizer estimates 120 rows will match the condition **survived = true**.
- The width of each row (in bytes), which helps PostgreSQL determine the memory usage for the query.

This sequential scan indicates that no index is being used, so the database has to scan the entire table to find rows where **survived = true**.

Now, to improve the performance of this query, we can add an index on the **survived** column. This will allow PostgreSQL to use an **index scan** instead of a sequential scan, which can significantly reduce query execution time for larger datasets.

- Create an Index on the `survived` column:

```
CREATE INDEX idx_survived ON titanic_data.passengers
(survived);
```

- Run `EXPLAIN` again:

```
EXPLAIN SELECT * FROM titanic_data.passengers WHERE
survived = true;
```

- The new output should look like this:

```
Bitmap Heap Scan on titanic_data.passengers
(cost=4.21..12.33 rows=120 width=70)

  Recheck Cond: (survived = true)

  ->  Bitmap Index Scan on idx_survived  (cost=0.00..4.21
rows=120 width=0)
```

In the above sample,

- PostgreSQL is now using an indexed scan to fetch the matching rows more efficiently.
- Bitmap index scan indicates that PostgreSQL is scanning the **idx_survived** index to quickly find the rows where **survived = true**.
- Costs and rows have changed, reflecting the reduced overhead due to the use of an index.

This improvement shows how creating an index can make the query more efficient by reducing the number of rows PostgreSQL needs to scan.

Using EXPLAIN ANALYZE to Measure Query Performance

While **EXPLAIN** shows the query execution plan and estimated costs, it doesn't provide actual runtime statistics. This is where **EXPLAIN ANALYZE** comes in. It executes the query and provides both the execution plan and real-time statistics, allowing you to see how long each operation took and whether the query planner's estimates were accurate.

To understand more better, we will run **EXPLAIN ANALYZE** on the same query after adding the index:

```
EXPLAIN ANALYZE SELECT * FROM titanic_data.passengers
WHERE survived = true;
```

This will output something like:

```
Bitmap Heap Scan on titanic_data.passengers
(cost=4.21..12.33 rows=120 width=70) (actual
time=0.054..0.078 rows=120 loops=1)

  Recheck Cond: (survived = true)

  Heap Blocks: exact=15

  ->  Bitmap Index Scan on idx_survived  (cost=0.00..4.21
rows=120 width=0) (actual time=0.026..0.026 rows=120
loops=1)

        Index Cond: (survived = true)

Planning Time: 0.203 ms
```

```
Execution Time: 0.125 ms
```

Here, in addition to the execution plan, we also see **actual execution times** and row counts:

- The **`actual time=0.054..0.078`** shows the time (in milliseconds) it took to execute this part of the query.
- The **`rows=120`** field indicates how many rows were returned from the query, matching the planner's estimate.
- The total execution time for the query is **`0.125 ms`**, a very fast query thanks to the index.

Using `EXPLAIN` to Optimize Complex Queries

We will move on to a more complex query involving a join between tables. We will use **EXPLAIN** to understand how PostgreSQL handles joins and aggregates, and we will look for potential optimizations.

Here, we want to find the total fare paid by passengers who survived, grouped by the class of travel (**pclass**):

```
EXPLAIN SELECT pclass, SUM(fare) FROM
titanic_data.passengers WHERE survived = true GROUP BY
pclass;
```

The output might look like this:

```
GroupAggregate  (cost=25.30..26.33 rows=3 width=12)

  Group Key: pclass

  ->  Sort  (cost=25.30..25.60 rows=120 width=4)

        Sort Key: pclass

        ->  Seq Scan on passengers  (cost=0.00..20.20
rows=120 width=4)

              Filter: (survived = true)
```

In the above, we see a few important operations:

- PostgreSQL is grouping the rows by **pclass** and aggregating the **fare** values.
- Before grouping, PostgreSQL sorts the rows by **pclass**.
- The sequential scan still appears because no index is being used to filter the rows where **survived = true**.

Now, to optimize this query, we will add an index on **pclass**:

```
CREATE INDEX idx_pclass ON titanic_data.passengers
(pclass);
```

Now, re-run the query with **EXPLAIN**:

```
EXPLAIN SELECT pclass, SUM(fare) FROM
titanic_data.passengers WHERE survived = true GROUP BY
pclass;
```

The result will show an improvement:

```
GroupAggregate  (cost=5.45..6.48 rows=3 width=12)

  Group Key: pclass

  ->  Bitmap Heap Scan on passengers  (cost=4.33..5.45
rows=120 width=4)

        Recheck Cond: (survived = true)

        ->  Bitmap Index Scan on idx_survived
(cost=0.00..4.33 rows=120 width=0)
```

In addition, the use of **EXPLAIN** and **EXPLAIN ANALYZE** can identify potential bottlenecks in query execution, such as:

- Sequential scans are fine for small tables, but for large tables, consider creating indexes to improve performance.
- Queries that involve sorting or grouping can benefit from indexes that match the **GROUP BY** or **ORDER BY** columns.

Resource Management Techniques

In this topic, we will implement **connection pooling** using **pgBouncer** and monitor query performance using **pg_stat_statements** to handle workloads effectively. These techniques help prevent overuse of system resources, especially in environments with many concurrent users or heavy query loads.

Connection Pooling with pgBouncer

When handling high numbers of client connections, managing resources can become inefficient. This is where **pgBouncer**, a lightweight connection pooler for PostgreSQL, comes into play. It maintains a pool of active database connections and reuses them, instead of opening a new connection for each client request, and thereby significantly reduces overhead, especially in environments with short-lived connections, such as web applications.

Installing pgBouncer

- Install the pgBouncer package:

```
sudo apt-get install pgBouncer
```

- Once installed, open the configuration file located in **`/etc/pgbouncer/pgbouncer.ini`**:

```
sudo nano /etc/pgbouncer/pgbouncer.ini
```

Then, you'll need to configure several key parameters for connection pooling.

Configuring pgBouncer

Within the **pgbouncer.ini** file, configure the following settings:

- Define the database that pgBouncer will manage. For example, to pool connections for our **`titanic_db`**:

```
[databases]

titanic_db = host=localhost port=5432 dbname=titanic_db
```

- Set the pooling mode. In most cases, **`transaction`** pooling is ideal as it allows each client to reuse a connection during a transaction:

```
pool_mode = transaction
```

In this mode, pgBouncer allocates connections to clients only for the duration of the transaction, returning the connection to the pool once the transaction completes.

- Then, configure the maximum number of connections pgBouncer will manage:

```
max_client_conn = 1000

default_pool_size = 20
```

This allows pgBouncer to handle up to 1,000 clients but only opens 20 active database connections at a time.

- Next, enable PostgreSQL authentication for pooled connections by setting the authentication type and specifying the location of the password file:

```
auth_type = md5

auth_file = /etc/pgbouncer/userlist.txt
```

The **`userlist.txt`** file contains user credentials that pgBouncer will use to authenticate incoming clients.

Starting and Monitoring pgBouncer

- Start the pgBouncer service:

```
sudo systemctl start pgbouncer
```

- You can monitor the pgBouncer pool using the following command:

```
psql -p 6432 -d pgbouncer -U postgres -c "SHOW POOLS"
```

This will provide insights into active client connections, pool size, and pool utilization.

Managing Workloads with **`pg_stat_statements`**

This **pg_stat_statements** extension allows you to view the execution statistics of all queries executed on the database, helping you identify slow or resource-intensive queries and optimize them for better performance.

Enabling 'pg_stat_statements'

Before using **pg_stat_statements**, you must enable the extension in your PostgreSQL instance.

- Open the **postgresql.conf** file, and enable the extension by adding the following line:

```
shared_preload_libraries = 'pg_stat_statements'
```

- Create the extension in the database:

```
CREATE EXTENSION pg_stat_statements;
```

Now, PostgreSQL is configured to track query execution statistics.

Using 'pg_stat_statements'

To view query statistics, use the following query to analyze the top queries by total execution time:

```
SELECT query, calls, total_time, rows, mean_time

FROM pg_stat_statements

ORDER BY total_time DESC

LIMIT 10;
```

Here,

- **query**: The SQL query that was executed.
- **calls**: The number of times the query was executed.
- **total_time**: The total time spent executing the query.
- **mean_time**: The average execution time of the query.

This will return a list of the most expensive queries, helping you identify bottlenecks.

Resetting Statistics

To reset the statistics collected by **pg_stat_statements**, run the following command:

```
SELECT pg_stat_statements_reset();
```

This is useful when you want to monitor performance over a specific period without the influence of previous queries.

Analyzing Slow Queries

Assume, we discover that a particular query is slow. We can use **pg_stat_statements** to get detailed information about it, and then use **EXPLAIN ANALYZE** to check how PostgreSQL is executing the query.

Check below:

```
EXPLAIN ANALYZE SELECT * FROM titanic_data.passengers
WHERE survived = true;
```

You can see if indexes are being used, how long each part of the query takes, and whether any parts of the query can be optimized.

Optimizing Queries based on Statistics

Once you've identified slow queries, you can take steps to optimize them:

- If the query frequently filters by certain columns (e.g., **`survived`**), create indexes to speed up retrieval.
- Consider rewriting the query to use more efficient joins, subqueries, or set operations.
- For complex queries that require sorting or joining large datasets, increase **`work_mem`** to provide more memory for these operations.

For example, if a query like:

```
SELECT * FROM titanic_data.passengers WHERE pclass = 3
ORDER BY fare DESC;
```

is identified as slow, then create an index on **pclass** and **fare** to significantly speed up its execution:

```
CREATE INDEX idx_pclass_fare ON titanic_data.passengers
(pclass, fare);
```

This will reduce the execution time by allowing PostgreSQL to use an index scan instead of a sequential scan.

By implementing **pgBouncer** for connection pooling, you can dramatically improve PostgreSQL's ability to handle high concurrency without overwhelming the system. In tandem, using **pg_stat_statements** provides powerful insights into query performance, enabling you to monitor, identify, and optimize slow or resource-intensive queries. Together, these techniques ensure PostgreSQL instance remains performant even under heavy loads.

Logging and Auditing

Logging helps track system performance, capture query execution details, and identify issues, while auditing is crucial for compliance, allowing you to track and review database activities, particularly related to security and sensitive data. To understand better, we will design a scenario for the Titanic dataset to demonstrate how logging and auditing can be configured logically for real-world use cases. And, this implementation will help monitor actions such as data access, changes to the schema, and any suspicious behavior.

Sample Program: Monitoring Passenger Data Queries

Imagine that the Titanic database contains sensitive passenger information, and it's crucial to monitor when queries are executed against the **passengers** table. You also want to track long-running queries that might degrade performance.

To achieve this, we will configure PostgreSQL to log:

- All queries executed on the **`passengers`** table.
- Queries that take longer than a certain threshold (e.g., 500 milliseconds).
- Any changes made to the schema, such as adding or modifying tables.

To set up logging, open the **postgresql.conf** file and modify the following parameters:

Enable Logging

Ensure that logging is enabled.

```
log_destination = 'csvlog'  # Output logs in CSV format

logging_collector = on  # Enable the logging collector

log_directory = 'pg_log'  # Directory for storing log
files
```

```
log_filename = 'postgresql-%Y-%m-%d_%H%M%S.log'  # Log
filename pattern
```

Log All Queries

To capture all queries that touch the **passengers** table, enable query logging.

```
log_statement = 'all'
```

This will log all SQL statements that are executed. However, for production environments, this can be expensive in terms of disk space and processing. In this case, consider using **log_min_duration_statement** to log only long-running queries.

Log Long-Running Queries

Set a threshold for logging queries that take longer than 500 milliseconds.

```
log_min_duration_statement = 500  # Log queries that take
longer than 500ms
```

This is useful for identifying queries that might need optimization.

Schema Changes Logging

To capture schema changes (such as **CREATE**, **ALTER**, or **DROP** operations), ensure **log_statement** is set to **ddl** (Data Definition Language) operations.

```
log_statement = 'ddl'  # Log schema changes
```

Log Connection and Disconnections

To track when users connect or disconnect from the database.

```
log_connections = on

log_disconnections = on
```

Log Client Information

Capture client information (IP address and port).

```
log_line_prefix = '%m [%p] %u@%d %r '  # Includes
timestamp, PID, user, database, and client IP
```

Once you've made these changes, restart PostgreSQL to apply them:

```
sudo systemctl restart postgresql@17-main
```

Reviewing the Logs

After logging is configured, PostgreSQL will create log files in the **pg_log** directory. Each log entry will contain details like the query, the time it took to execute, the client making the query, and the table being queried. This provides detailed visibility into how the database is being used.

For example, an entry in the log might look like this:

```
2024-09-25 12:30:45.123 [1234] alice@titanic_db
192.168.1.100 LOG:  duration: 750 ms  statement: SELECT *
FROM titanic_data.passengers WHERE survived = true;
```

This indicates that the query took 750 milliseconds to complete, which is above our threshold of 500 milliseconds. This can help identify queries that are slowing down the database.

Sample Program: Auditing Access to Passenger Data

While logging captures general database activity, **auditing** tracks specific actions, particularly those related to security or compliance. The **pgAudit** extension in PostgreSQL enables detailed auditing of database activities, including queries, modifications, and access to sensitive data. This is particularly useful for auditing data access in compliance with security policies.

Here, we assume the following:

- We need to audit any SELECT statements executed on the **`passengers`** table because it contains sensitive passenger information.
- We also want to audit any changes to the schema, such as creating, modifying, or deleting tables in the **`titanic_data`** schema.

Installing pgAudit

To implement auditing,

- First install pgAudit:

```
sudo apt-get install postgresql-contrib
```

- Enable pgAudit by modifying the **postgresql.conf** file to load the extension:

```
shared_preload_libraries = 'pgaudit'
```

- Restart PostgreSQL to apply the changes, and create the pgAudit extension in the Titanic database:

```
sudo systemctl restart postgresql@17-main

CREATE EXTENSION pgaudit;
```

Configuring pgAudit

Now that pgAudit is installed, we need to configure it to track specific actions in the **titanic_data** schema, especially on the **passengers** table. To audit SELECT statements and schema changes, we set the following configuration:

- Enable auditing for all read (**READ**) and write (**WRITE**) operations on the database:

```
SET pgaudit.log = 'read, write';
```

- Audit all **SELECT** queries on the **passengers** table:

```
ALTER TABLE titanic_data.passengers ENABLE ROW LEVEL
SECURITY;

CREATE POLICY audit_passengers_policy

ON titanic_data.passengers

FOR SELECT

USING (true);
```

This ensures that any **SELECT** query on the **passengers** table is logged for auditing purposes.

Reviewing Audit Logs

Once pgAudit is configured, all audited actions will be logged in the PostgreSQL log files. For example, if a user selects data from the **passengers** table, an audit entry might look like this:

```
2024-09-25 14:15:32.456 [2345] bob@titanic_db
192.168.1.105 AUDIT: SESSION, 1, SELECT, TABLE,
public.passengers, SELECT * FROM public.passengers WHERE
survived = true;
```

This log entry provides the following information:

- **Timestamp**: When the query was executed.
- **User and Database**: The user (**bob**) connected to the Titanic database.
- **Operation**: A **SELECT** statement was executed on the **passengers** table.
- **Details**: The exact query that was executed (**SELECT * FROM public.passengers WHERE survived = true**).

This allows administrators to track exactly who is accessing sensitive passenger data, which is crucial for compliance with data protection regulations.

We can also combine PostgreSQL's logging capabilities with the pgAudit extension to create a comprehensive monitoring and auditing framework. And, it is considered to be particularly useful in environments with strict compliance requirements, such as GDPR or HIPAA, where you need to audit data access and modifications.

Summary

In summary, our objective was clear: optimize PostgreSQL for enhanced performance and resource management. We started by learning how to optimize the server's performance through memory and resource allocation strategies. This included adjusting critical parameters such as shared_buffers, work_mem, and maintenance_work_mem to ensure efficient use of system resources and improve query execution times. We then examined query planning and execution, using EXPLAIN and EXPLAIN ANALYZE to understand how PostgreSQL's query optimizer chooses execution plans. By analyzing query costs and execution times, we swiftly identified and resolved potential bottlenecks, optimizing queries by creating indexes and adjusting query logic.

Next, we implemented resource management techniques using pgBouncer for connection pooling. Furthermore, we leveraged pg_stat_statements to monitor and manage query performance, swiftly identifying and optimizing slow-running queries for enhanced efficiency. Finally, we set up advanced logging and auditing, focusing on tracking database activity and security-related actions. We configured PostgreSQL's logging capabilities to capture long-running queries and schema changes, and we implemented pgAudit to monitor sensitive data access in the Titanic database.

CHAPTER 5: EFFECTIVE DATA MANAGEMENT

Brief Overview

This chapter provides indispensable techniques for effective data management. We start with Advanced Data Types and Extensions, where you will master PostgreSQL's powerful data types, including JSONB, arrays, and composite types. You will also learn about useful extensions like pg_trgm for text search. Next, we'll dive into Bulk Data Operations. You'll learn how to efficiently load, import, and manipulate large amounts of data using commands like COPY. These operations are essential for handling large datasets. You will also learn how to create and manage advanced indexes like GIN, GiST, and BRIN indexes in our section on sophisticated indexing techniques.

Finally, we will dive into constraints, triggers, and functions. You will learn how to enforce data integrity through constraints, automate processes using triggers, and build complex logic within your database using functions. These tools are the key to intelligent database management, ensuring that your data remains consistent and reliable throughout its lifecycle.

Advanced Data Types and Extensions

Working with JSONB

PostgreSQL's **JSONB** data type allows us to store JSON (JavaScript Object Notation) data in a binary format, making it more efficient for querying and indexing than the plain JSON data type. JSONB is particularly useful when working with semi-structured data, such as log data or API responses.

To understand better, we will add a new column to the **passengers** table to store additional information about each passenger in a JSONB format, such as their **passport information** and **ticket details**.

Alter Table to Add JSONB Column

```
ALTER TABLE titanic_data.passengers ADD COLUMN details
JSONB;
```

Inserting JSONB Data

Now, we insert some data for one of the passengers. This JSONB object will store their passport information and ticket details.

```
UPDATE titanic_data.passengers
```

```
SET details = '{"passport": "P123456", "ticket": {"type": "First-Class", "price": 150.00}}'

WHERE id = 1;
```

Querying JSONB Data

To query data inside the JSONB column, PostgreSQL provides a variety of operators and functions. For example, to find all passengers with a first-class ticket:

```
SELECT name, details

FROM titanic_data.passengers

WHERE details -> 'ticket' ->> 'type' = 'First-Class';
```

In the above, **->** is used to access a JSON object field, and **->>** extracts the field value as text. This query efficiently retrieves all passengers with a ticket type of "First-Class."

Indexing JSONB Data

To optimize performance, especially when querying specific JSON fields frequently, we can create a **GIN (Generalized Inverted Index)** on the **details** column:

```
CREATE INDEX idx_passengers_details ON titanic_data.passengers USING GIN (details);
```

This GIN index improves the performance of queries that search within the JSONB column, making it faster to retrieve data like the example above.

Working with Arrays

PostgreSQL arrays allow you to store multiple values of the same data type in a single column. Arrays are useful when you need to represent a list of items related to a single record, such as multiple phone numbers, interests, or, in our case, the list of destinations for a passenger's trip.

Here, we will add a column to the **passengers** table to store the multiple destinations each passenger plans to visit.

Alter Table to Add Array Column

```
ALTER TABLE titanic_data.passengers ADD COLUMN
destinations TEXT[];
```

Inserting Array Data

Now, we insert data for a passenger who has multiple planned destinations:

```
UPDATE titanic_data.passengers

SET destinations = ARRAY['Paris', 'New York', 'London']

WHERE id = 2;
```

The **ARRAY[ ]** syntax allows us to insert multiple values into the array column.

Querying Array Data

To query passengers who are planning to visit a specific destination, we can use the **ANY** operator:

```
SELECT name, destinations

FROM titanic_data.passengers

WHERE 'Paris' = ANY (destinations);
```

This query will return all passengers who have "Paris" listed in their destinations array.

Manipulating Arrays

PostgreSQL provides array-specific functions for manipulation. For example, if you want to add a new destination to a passenger's array:

```
UPDATE titanic_data.passengers

SET destinations = array_append(destinations, 'Tokyo')

WHERE id = 2;
```

This appends "Tokyo" to the existing list of destinations.

Working with Composite Types

A **composite type** in PostgreSQL is a custom data type made up of multiple fields, similar to a structured object in programming. Composite types allow you to represent related data in a more structured format, which is especially useful for representing objects with multiple attributes, such as an address.

To do this, we will create a composite type to represent passenger addresses, including fields like street, city, state, and zip code.

Create Composite Type

```
CREATE TYPE address AS (
  street VARCHAR(100),
  city VARCHAR(50),
  state VARCHAR(50),
  zip_code VARCHAR(10)
);
```

Add Composite Type as a Column

We can now add an **address** column to the **passengers** table using the newly defined composite type:

```
ALTER TABLE titanic_data.passengers ADD COLUMN address
address;
```

Inserting Data into Composite Type

We will insert data into this new column for a specific passenger:

```
UPDATE titanic_data.passengers
SET address = ('123 Main St', 'New York', 'NY', '10001')
WHERE id = 3;
```

In the above, the data for the composite type is passed as a tuple (set of values).

Querying Composite Types

To retrieve data from the composite column, we can use dot notation to access individual fields:

```
SELECT name, address.city, address.state

FROM titanic_data.passengers

WHERE id = 3;
```

This query will return the passenger's name along with their city and state.

Using 'hstore' and 'pg_trgm'

PostgreSQL supports several extensions that provide additional functionality for working with specific data types. Two notable extensions are **hstore** and **pg_trgm**.

The **hstore** extension allows you to store key-value pairs in a single column, making it an alternative to using JSON for certain use cases. It's particularly useful when you need a flexible schema that can accommodate dynamic attributes for records.

Install and Enable 'hstore'

Before using **`hstore`**, you need to install and enable the extension:

```
CREATE EXTENSION hstore;
```

Adding 'hstore' Data

Now, you want to store additional attributes for passengers, such as dietary preferences or medical conditions. We can add an **`hstore`** column to store this key-value data.

```
ALTER TABLE titanic_data.passengers ADD COLUMN
preferences hstore;
```

Inserting Data

To insert key-value pairs into the **`preferences`** column:

```
UPDATE titanic_data.passengers
```

```
SET preferences = 'diet' => 'vegetarian', 'medical' =>
'none'

WHERE id = 4;
```

Querying 'hstore' Data

To query passengers with specific preferences, such as those with vegetarian diets:

```
SELECT name, preferences

FROM titanic_data.passengers

WHERE preferences->'diet' = 'vegetarian';
```

The **pg_trgm** extension provides functionality for **fuzzy text searching** using trigram similarity. This is particularly useful when you want to find records based on partial matches, spelling errors, or approximate matches.

Install and Enable 'pg_trgm'

First, enable the **`pg_trgm`** extension:

```
CREATE EXTENSION pg_trgm;
```

Using 'pg_trgm' for Fuzzy Search

We will implement a scenario where a user wants to search for passengers with names that closely match "Jon Doe," even if there are minor spelling variations.

```
SELECT name

FROM titanic_data.passengers

WHERE name % 'Jon Doe';
```

The **`%`** operator, provided by **`pg_trgm`**, returns rows where the name is similar to the provided string based on trigram similarity.

Creating Index for Fuzzy Search

To speed up the fuzzy search, create a **GIN index** on the **name** column:

```
CREATE INDEX idx_passengers_name_trgm ON
titanic_data.passengers USING GIN (name gin_trgm_ops);
```

This index optimizes searches that use the **%** operator, making them more efficient for large datasets.

These advanced data types along with extensions are very easily able to manage complex and unstructured data more efficiently. These tools provide flexibility, enabling you to store, query, and manipulate data in ways that suit various real-world applications.

Sophisticated Indexing Techniques

Indexing techniques can drastically reduce query execution times, particularly when dealing with unstructured data, text search, or large partitions. While B-tree indexes are the default and most commonly used, PostgreSQL offers advanced indexing methods like **GIN**, **GiST**, and **BRIN**, which are tailored for specific data types and query patterns.

Here, we will experience these advanced indexing techniques and also cover how to perform index maintenance and monitoring to ensure database performance remains optimal over time.

GIN (Generalized Inverted Index)

GIN (Generalized Inverted Index) is a powerful indexing method for handling multi-valued data, such as arrays, JSONB, or full-text search. It allows you to search for elements within these complex data types efficiently.

In our Titanic database, we previously added a **details** column in JSONB format to the **passengers** table. We will now create a GIN index on the **details** column to improve search performance when querying specific fields within the JSONB data.

Creating GIN Index

To create a GIN index on the **details** JSONB column:

```
CREATE INDEX idx_passengers_details_gin ON
titanic_data.passengers USING GIN (details);
```

This GIN index allows PostgreSQL to efficiently search inside the JSONB structure.

Querying with GIN Index

We will run a query to find all passengers who have a first-class ticket stored in their **details**:

```
SELECT name, details
FROM titanic_data.passengers
WHERE details @> '{"ticket": {"type": "First-Class"}}';
```

The **@>** operator checks whether the JSONB object on the left contains the key-value pairs specified on the right. The GIN index we created accelerates this query by making it unnecessary for PostgreSQL to perform a full table scan.

Maintaining GIN Indexes

Like other indexes, GIN indexes require regular maintenance to ensure their efficiency. Over time, as data is inserted, updated, or deleted, GIN indexes can become bloated, which may slow down query performance. To address this, PostgreSQL provides the **REINDEX** command:

```
REINDEX INDEX idx_passengers_details_gin;
```

Running this command rebuilds the index, removing any bloat and ensuring it remains efficient.

GiST (Generalized Search Tree)

GiST (Generalized Search Tree) is a flexible indexing framework that supports a wide variety of data types, including geometric data, full-text search, and range types. It is especially useful for indexing spatial data and performing searches on non-exact matches, such as range queries or similarity searches.

Now, we have a **coordinates** column in the **passengers** table that stores the geographic location of passengers' departure points. We can create a GiST index on this column to speed up queries that involve spatial data.

Adding Geometric Data Column

First, we add a **coordinates** column to store passenger departure points as geometric data (using the **point** data type):

```
ALTER TABLE titanic_data.passengers ADD COLUMN
coordinates POINT;
```

Inserting Geometric Data

We will insert some sample data for a passenger:

```
UPDATE titanic_data.passengers

SET coordinates = POINT(40.7128, -74.0060)  --
Coordinates for New York

WHERE id = 1;
```

Creating GiST Index

Now, we can create a GiST index on the **coordinates** column:

```
CREATE INDEX idx_passengers_coordinates_gist ON
titanic_data.passengers USING GiST (coordinates);
```

Querying with GiST Index

To find all passengers who departed from a location within 10 units of a specific point, we can use a query like this:

```
SELECT name, coordinates

FROM titanic_data.passengers

WHERE coordinates <@> POINT(40.7128, -74.0060) < 10;
```

The **<@>** operator calculates the distance between two points, and the GiST index optimizes this spatial query by quickly identifying points within the specified range.

BRIN (Block Range INdex)

BRIN (Block Range INdex) is designed for very large, sequentially ordered datasets. Unlike B-tree, GIN, or GiST indexes, which index individual rows, BRIN indexes summarize entire blocks of data. This makes them extremely space-efficient but suitable only for queries where the data is naturally ordered, such as timestamps or sequential IDs.

Now, here think that the Titanic database contains a large number of passenger records, and we want to create a BRIN index on the **age** column, which is likely to be somewhat sequential. BRIN indexes are ideal for cases where we don't need precise row-level indexing but still want to speed up range queries.

Creating BRIN Index

To create a BRIN index on the **age** column:

```
CREATE INDEX idx_passengers_age_brin ON
titanic_data.passengers USING BRIN (age);
```

This BRIN index summarizes blocks of data, significantly reducing storage space while still improving query performance for large datasets.

Querying with BRIN Index

When querying passengers based on age ranges, BRIN indexes are highly efficient. For example, to find all passengers aged between 30 and 50:

```
SELECT name, age

FROM titanic_data.passengers

WHERE age BETWEEN 30 AND 50;
```

BRIN will quickly narrow down the blocks that may contain rows matching this condition, reducing the need to scan irrelevant data.

Maintaining BRIN Indexes

Although BRIN indexes are relatively maintenance-free compared to other index types, it's still a good practice to periodically use the **VACUUM** command to ensure that the blocks remain compact and properly summarized:

```
VACUUM ANALYZE titanic_data.passengers;
```

This ensures that the BRIN index continues to perform well, even as the data grows.

Index Maintenance and Monitoring

Indexes requires regular monitoring and maintenance to ensure they don't degrade performance over time due to bloat or inefficient query patterns. And, PostgreSQL provides several tools to monitor index usage and maintain them effectively.

Monitoring Index Usage

PostgreSQL's **pg_stat_user_indexes** view allows you to monitor index usage statistics. This view provides information on how often each index is used for queries, helping you identify unused or underused indexes that may be candidates for removal.

To see how often each index on the **passengers** table is being used, run the following query:

```
SELECT indexrelname, idx_scan, idx_tup_read,
idx_tup_fetch

FROM pg_stat_user_indexes

WHERE relname = 'passengers';
```

Here,

- **idx_scan**: The number of index scans (i.e., how often the index was used).
- **idx_tup_read**: The number of rows the index helped retrieve.
- **idx_tup_fetch**: The number of rows the index helped fetch from the table.

If an index has a low **idx_scan** value, it may not be useful, and you might consider removing it.

Rebuilding and Removing Indexes

If an index has become bloated or inefficient, you can **rebuild** it using the **REINDEX** command. However, if an index is rarely used, removing it might improve overall database performance by reducing overhead.

To rebuild an index on the **passengers** table:

```
REINDEX INDEX idx_passengers_age_brin;
```

If an index is no longer useful, you can drop it:

```
DROP INDEX idx_passengers_details_gin;
```

This approach ensures that only useful indexes are kept, while underperforming ones are either rebuilt or removed.

Constraints, Triggers, and Functions

Constraints, **triggers**, and **functions** are powerful tools for enforcing data integrity, automating database tasks, and embedding logic directly within the database. These mechanisms allow you to maintain consistency, enforce business rules, and handle complex workflows at the database level, without relying entirely on external application logic. Now here, we will build upon the previously demonstrated example to show how to create complex constraints, write advanced triggers, and design stored functions.

Sample Program: Creating Complex Constraints

Constraints enforce rules at the database level, ensuring that only valid data enters a table. PostgreSQL supports various types of constraints, such as **CHECK**, **NOT NULL**, **UNIQUE**, and **FOREIGN KEY** constraints, which can be combined to handle complex requirements.

In the Titanic dataset, we assume we want to ensure that:

- The **age** column cannot contain negative values.
- Children under the age of 16 cannot have a "First-Class" ticket.

We can accomplish this using a **CHECK constraint**.

Adding a **CHECK** *Constraint on Age*

To ensure that the **age** column contains only non-negative values:

```
ALTER TABLE titanic_data.passengers

ADD CONSTRAINT age_check CHECK (age >= 0);
```

This constraint ensures that no record with a negative **age** value can be inserted.

Adding a **CHECK** *Constraint for Age and Ticket Type*

Next, we will add a constraint that ensures children under 16 do not have a "First-Class" ticket. Assuming the ticket class is stored in the **details** JSONB column:

```
ALTER TABLE titanic_data.passengers

ADD CONSTRAINT child_first_class_check CHECK (

  (details -> 'ticket' ->> 'type' != 'First-Class') OR
(age >= 16)
```

```
);
```

This constraint enforces that either the passenger's ticket is not "First-Class" or their age is 16 or older.

Testing Constraints

To test this, try inserting a passenger with an invalid age or ticket class combination:

```
INSERT INTO titanic_data.passengers (name, age, details)

VALUES ('Test Child', 12, '{"ticket": {"type": "First-Class", "price": 100.00}}');
```

This insert will fail due to the **CHECK** constraint, preventing invalid data from entering the database.

Sample Program: Writing Advanced Triggers

Triggers are functions that are automatically executed (or "triggered") by specific events on a table, such as **INSERT**, **UPDATE**, or **DELETE** operations. Triggers are useful for automating tasks such as logging changes, enforcing additional constraints, or updating related records.

Now, here consider that we want to log any changes to the **passengers** table into a separate **passenger_log** table. This log should capture the **old and new data** whenever a passenger's details are updated.

Create the Log Table

First, create a **passenger_log** table to store changes:

```
CREATE TABLE titanic_data.passenger_log (

  log_id SERIAL PRIMARY KEY,

  passenger_id INT,

  old_data JSONB,

  new_data JSONB,

  changed_at TIMESTAMP DEFAULT NOW()
```

```
);
```

This table will capture the old and new data, along with the time the change was made.

Create a Trigger Function

Next, write a trigger function that will log the old and new values whenever a passenger's details are updated:

```
CREATE OR REPLACE FUNCTION log_passenger_changes()
RETURNS TRIGGER AS $$

BEGIN

  INSERT INTO titanic_data.passenger_log (passenger_id,
old_data, new_data)

  VALUES (OLD.id, to_jsonb(OLD), to_jsonb(NEW));

  RETURN NEW;

END;

$$ LANGUAGE plpgsql;
```

This function will insert the old and new row data into the **passenger_log** table every time an update is made.

Create the Trigger

Finally, create a trigger that executes this function before every update on the **passengers** table:

```
CREATE TRIGGER passenger_update_trigger

BEFORE UPDATE ON titanic_data.passengers

FOR EACH ROW

EXECUTE FUNCTION log_passenger_changes();
```

Testing the Trigger

To test the trigger, update a passenger's details:

```
UPDATE titanic_data.passengers

SET age = 25, details = '{"ticket": {"type": "Second-Class", "price": 100.00}}'

WHERE id = 1;
```

After executing this query, check the **passenger_log** table to see the old and new data captured by the trigger:

```
SELECT * FROM titanic_data.passenger_log;
```

The log table will display the previous and updated data, allowing you to track changes to the **passengers** table over time.

Sample Program: Designing Stored Functions

Stored functions in PostgreSQL allow you to encapsulate complex logic and reuse it across multiple queries or triggers. Functions can return scalar values, sets, or even custom types, making them highly versatile.

For this, we will create a stored function to calculate the total revenue generated from ticket sales based on the **ticket** details stored in the JSONB **details** column.

Create the Function

The following function will calculate the total revenue by summing up the ticket prices from the **passengers** table:

```
CREATE OR REPLACE FUNCTION calculate_total_revenue()
RETURNS NUMERIC AS $$

DECLARE

  total NUMERIC := 0;

BEGIN
```

```
  SELECT SUM((details -> 'ticket' ->> 'price')::NUMERIC)
INTO total

  FROM titanic_data.passengers;

  RETURN total;

END;

$$ LANGUAGE plpgsql;
```

This function extracts the **price** field from the JSONB **details** column, converts it to a numeric value, and sums it across all rows in the **passengers** table.

Using the Function

To calculate the total revenue, simply call the function:

```
SELECT calculate_total_revenue();
```

This will return the total sum of all ticket prices.

Creating a Function with Parameters

Next, we create a stored function that accepts a passenger ID and returns the ticket price for that passenger. The following function retrieves the ticket price for a given passenger ID:

```
CREATE OR REPLACE FUNCTION get_ticket_price(passenger_id
INT) RETURNS NUMERIC AS $$

DECLARE

  ticket_price NUMERIC;

BEGIN

  SELECT (details -> 'ticket' ->> 'price')::NUMERIC INTO
ticket_price

  FROM titanic_data.passengers
```

```
    WHERE id = passenger_id;

    RETURN ticket_price;

END;

$$ LANGUAGE plpgsql;
```

To retrieve the ticket price for a specific passenger, call the function and pass the passenger ID as an argument:

```
SELECT get_ticket_price(1);
```

This will return the ticket price for the passenger with ID 1.

Combining Constraints, Triggers, and Functions

We can also create powerful automation and validation rules within your database, if we combine al these tools together. Given below is a final example that combines constraints, triggers, and functions:

- We will add a **constraint** that checks that the ticket price is not negative.
- We will create a **trigger** that automatically recalculates the total ticket revenue whenever a new passenger is added or updated.
- We will use the **stored function `calculate_total_revenue`** to compute the total ticket revenue.

Add a Constraint for Ticket Price

```
ALTER TABLE titanic_data.passengers

ADD CONSTRAINT ticket_price_check CHECK ((details ->
'ticket' ->> 'price')::NUMERIC >= 0);
```

Create a Trigger to Recalculate Revenue on Insert/Update

```
CREATE OR REPLACE FUNCTION update_total_revenue() RETURNS
TRIGGER AS $$
```

```
BEGIN
  PERFORM calculate_total_revenue();
  RETURN NEW;
END;
$$ LANGUAGE plpgsql;

CREATE TRIGGER revenue_update_trigger
AFTER INSERT OR UPDATE ON titanic_data.passengers
FOR EACH ROW
EXECUTE FUNCTION update_total_revenue();
```

Now, every time a passenger's ticket details are added or updated, the trigger will call the **calculate_total_revenue** function to recalculate the total ticket revenue. The use of **complex constraints**, **advanced triggers**, and **stored functions** automates intricate database processes, ensuring data integrity and enforcing business rules directly within your PostgreSQL instance.

Summary

In a nutshell, we mastered the key aspects of effective data management in PostgreSQL. We worked with advanced data types, bulk operations, indexing techniques, and mechanisms to enforce data integrity. We started by learning how to use advanced data types like JSONB, arrays, and composite types. Next, we focused on bulk data operations, where we mastered the efficient handling of large datasets. We learned how to import or manipulate data using PostgreSQL's powerful commands in a quick and effective manner. We also implemented sophisticated indexing techniques using GIN, GiST, and BRIN indexes.

Finally, we automated database logic and enforced data integrity using complex constraints, triggers, and functions. This chapter covered essential skills for maintaining and managing PostgreSQL databases efficiently, with a focus on practical implementations using the Titanic dataset.

Chapter 6: Table Partitioning Strategies

Brief Overview

In this chapter, we will master table partitioning strategies in PostgreSQL. We will start by grasping the concepts of partitioning, seeing how it works in PostgreSQL, and understanding the benefits it offers, including improving query response times and reducing maintenance overhead.

Next, we will show you exactly how to implement partitioned tables. You will learn the ins and outs of different partitioning methods, including range, list, and hash partitioning. You will also learn how to apply these methods to real-world scenarios, including how to partition the Titanic dataset based on attributes like age or ticket class. We will then move on to managing partitions effectively, which includes tasks like adding, removing, or merging partitions as the dataset grows. You will also learn how to maintain partitions by reorganizing or cleaning up unused data, ensuring that your database runs efficiently.

Finally, we will optimize queries on partitioned tables. You will learn how PostgreSQL performs partition pruning, an optimization technique that skips irrelevant partitions, speeding up queries. We will also show you the best indexing strategies for partitioned tables, ensuring that even complex queries run quickly.

Partitioning Concepts

In PostgreSQL 17, partitioning has received notable updates, further enhancing its flexibility and management capabilities. One of the most significant improvements is the introduction of **partition merging and splitting**. This allows administrators to manage partitions more effectively by either combining partitions when they grow too small or splitting them when they become too large. For example, a partitioned table holding data from several years can now have a year-based partition split into quarters, improving performance when querying recent data. Similarly, merging partitions with low activity helps reduce overhead. These operations are achieved using the new **ALTER TABLE ... SPLIT PARTITION** and **ALTER TABLE ... MERGE PARTITIONS** commands.

Additionally, PostgreSQL experts have been discussing the benefits and trade-offs of partitioning strategies in this latest version. While partitioning is primarily viewed as a performance optimization technique, it is also increasingly recognized for simplifying data management in large databases. Experts have highlighted that partitioning can reduce the size of indexes, improve query planning by enabling partition pruning, and facilitate better management of large datasets over time. However, they also note that careful planning is essential to avoid unnecessary locking during partition management operations like splits and merges, which could temporarily block access to the parent table.

Implementing Partitioned Tables

Partitioning in PostgreSQL allows large tables to be broken down into smaller, more manageable parts called partitions. These partitions improve performance by enabling PostgreSQL to scan only the relevant sections of a table, rather than the entire dataset. Partitioning is particularly useful for large datasets like the Titanic passenger data, which can benefit from better query performance and easier maintenance.

Here, we will implement **Range**, **List**, and **Hash** partitioning on the Titanic dataset, illustrating how each method can be applied depending on the data and the queries being run.

Sample Program: Partitioning by Range

Range partitioning divides a table into partitions based on a range of values in a specified column. This method is ideal when you have data that naturally falls into specific ranges, such as dates, ages, or numerical values.

We will partition the Titanic dataset by the **age** of the passengers, placing passengers in different partitions based on age ranges. This can help optimize queries that frequently filter passengers by age.

Creating a Partitioned Table

First, create a partitioned table for the **`passengers`** dataset, specifying the **`age`** column for range partitioning:

```
CREATE TABLE titanic_data.passengers_partitioned (

    id SERIAL PRIMARY KEY,

    name VARCHAR(100),

    age INT,

    gender VARCHAR(10),

    survived BOOLEAN,

    details JSONB

) PARTITION BY RANGE (age);
```

This command creates the base **`passengers_partitioned`** table, but it doesn't contain any data. We will now create partitions that will hold data within specific age ranges.

Creating Range Partitions

We will create partitions for passengers based on age ranges:

- A partition for passengers under 18 (children).
- A partition for passengers between 18 and 60 (adults).
- A partition for passengers above 60 (seniors).

```
CREATE TABLE titanic_data.passengers_children PARTITION
OF titanic_data.passengers_partitioned

FOR VALUES FROM (0) TO (18);


CREATE TABLE titanic_data.passengers_adults PARTITION OF
titanic_data.passengers_partitioned

FOR VALUES FROM (18) TO (60);


CREATE TABLE titanic_data.passengers_seniors PARTITION OF
titanic_data.passengers_partitioned

FOR VALUES FROM (60) TO (150);
```

Inserting Data into the Partitioned Table

When inserting data, PostgreSQL automatically places each row in the appropriate partition based on the **age** value:

```
INSERT INTO titanic_data.passengers_partitioned (name,
age, gender, survived, details)

VALUES ('John Doe', 25, 'male', true, '{"ticket":
{"type": "First-Class", "price": 100.00}}'),

       ('Jane Doe', 12, 'female', false, '{"ticket":
{"type": "Second-Class", "price": 50.00}}'),
```

```
    ('Emily Smith', 65, 'female', true, '{"ticket":
{"type": "First-Class", "price": 200.00}}');
```

PostgreSQL will place each row into the appropriate partition: **passengers_children**, **passengers_adults**, or **passengers_seniors**.

Querying the Partitioned Table

When running queries that filter by age, PostgreSQL will use **partition pruning** to scan only the relevant partition, improving performance. For example:

```
SELECT * FROM titanic_data.passengers_partitioned WHERE
age BETWEEN 18 AND 60;
```

This query will only scan the **passengers_adults** partition, skipping the other partitions, thus reducing the query execution time.

Sample Program: Partitioning by List

List partitioning allows you to partition a table based on a discrete set of values. It is useful when you have a limited number of distinct values in a column, such as categories or types.

We will partition the Titanic data based on the **ticket class** (**First-Class**, **Second-Class**, **Third-Class**). This method is ideal for queries that filter data by ticket class, such as analyzing survival rates by class.

Creating a Partitioned Table

First, create a partitioned table that will hold passengers based on their ticket class, stored in the **details** JSONB field:

```
CREATE TABLE titanic_data.passengers_by_class (

    id SERIAL PRIMARY KEY,

    name VARCHAR(100),

    age INT,

    gender VARCHAR(10),
```

```
    survived BOOLEAN,
    details JSONB
) PARTITION BY LIST ((details ->> 'ticket' ->> 'type'));
```

This command tells PostgreSQL to partition the table based on the **ticket** type stored in the JSONB **details** column.

Creating List Partitions

Next, create partitions for each ticket class:

```
CREATE TABLE titanic_data.passengers_first_class
PARTITION OF titanic_data.passengers_by_class
FOR VALUES IN ('First-Class');


CREATE TABLE titanic_data.passengers_second_class
PARTITION OF titanic_data.passengers_by_class
FOR VALUES IN ('Second-Class');


CREATE TABLE titanic_data.passengers_third_class
PARTITION OF titanic_data.passengers_by_class
FOR VALUES IN ('Third-Class');
```

Inserting Data into the Partitioned Table

Insert passenger data with different ticket classes:

```
INSERT INTO titanic_data.passengers_by_class (name, age,
gender, survived, details)
```

```
VALUES ('Sarah Williams', 30, 'female', true, '{"ticket":
{"type": "First-Class", "price": 120.00}}'),

       ('Tom Brown', 40, 'male', false, '{"ticket":
{"type": "Third-Class", "price": 30.00}}'),

       ('Anna White', 22, 'female', true, '{"ticket":
{"type": "Second-Class", "price": 70.00}}');
```

PostgreSQL will automatically place each row into the correct partition based on the ticket type.

Querying the Partitioned Table

When querying for passengers in a specific ticket class, PostgreSQL will only scan the relevant partition:

```
SELECT * FROM titanic_data.passengers_by_class WHERE
details ->> 'ticket' ->> 'type' = 'First-Class';
```

This query will only scan the **passengers_first_class** partition, skipping the others.

Sample Program: Partitioning by Hash

Hash partitioning divides a table into partitions based on a hash function applied to the values of a specified column. This method ensures even distribution of data across partitions, making it useful when you don't have natural ranges or discrete categories but still want to improve performance by splitting data.

We will partition the Titanic dataset based on the **id** of passengers, ensuring that data is evenly distributed across partitions regardless of the ID values.

Creating a Partitioned Table

First, create a partitioned table that uses **id** as the partition key:

```
CREATE TABLE titanic_data.passengers_hash_partitioned (

    id SERIAL PRIMARY KEY,

    name VARCHAR(100),
```

```
    age INT,
    gender VARCHAR(10),
    survived BOOLEAN,
    details JSONB
) PARTITION BY HASH (id);
```

Creating Hash Partitions

Next, create multiple partitions to hold data distributed by the hash of the **id** column. We will create 4 partitions:

```
CREATE TABLE titanic_data.passengers_hash_0 PARTITION OF
titanic_data.passengers_hash_partitioned
FOR VALUES WITH (MODULUS 4, REMAINDER 0);

CREATE TABLE titanic_data.passengers_hash_1 PARTITION OF
titanic_data.passengers_hash_partitioned
FOR VALUES WITH (MODULUS 4, REMAINDER 1);

CREATE TABLE titanic_data.passengers_hash_2 PARTITION OF
titanic_data.passengers_hash_partitioned
FOR VALUES WITH (MODULUS 4, REMAINDER 2);

CREATE TABLE titanic_data.passengers_hash_3 PARTITION OF
titanic_data.passengers_hash_partitioned
FOR VALUES WITH (MODULUS 4, REMAINDER 3);
```

These partitions evenly distribute the rows across 4 partitions based on the **id** hash modulo operation.

Inserting Data into the Partitioned Table

When you insert data into the table, PostgreSQL automatically computes the hash of the **id** and places the row in the appropriate partition:

```
INSERT INTO titanic_data.passengers_hash_partitioned
(name, age, gender, survived, details)

VALUES ('James Black', 55, 'male', true, '{"ticket":
{"type": "First-Class", "price": 150.00}}');
```

Querying the Partitioned Table

Queries on this table are spread across partitions, which improves performance when the data grows large. For example:

```
SELECT * FROM titanic_data.passengers_hash_partitioned
WHERE id = 3;
```

PostgreSQL will only scan the partition containing the hash result for **id = 3**, optimizing the query.

By now, we implemented **range**, **list**, and **hash partitioning** methods on the Titanic dataset to optimize performance and better manage large datasets. Each of these partitioning methods can be applied based on the nature of the data and query patterns, allowing PostgreSQL to skip scanning irrelevant partitions, reducing the overhead, and improving query performance. This strategy is especially useful for large datasets like the Titanic dataset, where we frequently filter and query specific segments of data.

Managing Partitions Effectively

After implementing partitioning on the Titanic dataset, managing those partitions becomes essential as data grows or changes over time. PostgreSQL 17 introduces flexible partition management features, such as the ability to **add**, **merge**, and **split** partitions. These capabilities are useful when handling changes in data size or query requirements, ensuring that your partitions remain optimal for performance and manageability.

Here, we will demonstrate how to add new partitions as your data grows, merge smaller partitions for efficiency, and split large partitions to better manage increasing data.

Sample Program: Adding Partitions

As your data grows, you may need to add new partitions to accommodate future entries. For instance, if we are storing passengers by **age** or **ticket class**, we might anticipate new data that doesn't fit within the existing partitions, and therefore, additional partitions are required.

In our **range partitioned** Titanic table (partitioned by age), suppose we want to add a new partition for **infants** (passengers aged 0 to 1 year old), as this data is currently being grouped with children (ages 0-18).

Add a New Range Partition for Infants

We can easily add a new partition to handle infant passengers:

```
CREATE TABLE titanic_data.passengers_infants PARTITION OF
titanic_data.passengers_partitioned

FOR VALUES FROM (0) TO (1);
```

This command creates a new partition that will store all passengers aged between 0 and 1. Any new data inserted with **`age = 0`** or **`age = 1`** will now be placed in the **`passengers_infants`** partition, improving the specificity of our data management.

Verify the New Partition

You can verify that the partition was created successfully by checking the list of partitions under the **`passengers_partitioned`** table:

```
\d+ titanic_data.passengers_partitioned
```

This will show the newly added partition along with the existing ones.

Sample Program: Merging Partitions

Over time, some partitions may become too small or may no longer need to be separated. Merging these smaller partitions into larger ones can reduce the overhead of maintaining many partitions and improve query performance. PostgreSQL 17 allows you to merge partitions for better efficiency.

Here, we will decide that managing a separate partition for infants isn't necessary, and we want to merge it back with the **passengers_children** partition (ages 0-18).

Merge Partitions

To merge the **passengers_infants** partition back into the **passengers_children** partition, you would need to:

- Move data from the `passengers_infants` partition into the `passengers_children` partition.
- Drop the `passengers_infants` partition after the data transfer.

Following is how you can perform this operation:

```
INSERT INTO titanic_data.passengers_children

SELECT * FROM titanic_data.passengers_infants;



DROP TABLE titanic_data.passengers_infants;
```

This process moves all data from the **passengers_infants** partition into the **passengers_children** partition and then drops the now unnecessary partition.

Validate the Data Movement

After merging, check that the data has been moved and that the **passengers_infants** partition no longer exists by running:

```
SELECT * FROM titanic_data.passengers_children WHERE age
BETWEEN 0 AND 1;
```

This will confirm that infant passengers are now stored within the **passengers_children** partition.

Sample Program: Splitting Partitions

Splitting partitions can be necessary when a particular partition grows too large. For example, if the **adults** partition (ages 18-60) has grown significantly, you might want to split it into smaller sub-partitions to distribute the data more effectively and improve query performance.

Suppose we decide to split the **adults** partition into smaller partitions by decade to optimize queries based on age groups such as 18-30, 31-45, and 46-60.

Create New Partitions for Age Groups

We will create three new partitions to replace the original **passengers_adults** partition:

```
CREATE TABLE titanic_data.passengers_adults_18_30
PARTITION OF titanic_data.passengers_partitioned

FOR VALUES FROM (18) TO (31);


CREATE TABLE titanic_data.passengers_adults_31_45
PARTITION OF titanic_data.passengers_partitioned

FOR VALUES FROM (31) TO (46);


CREATE TABLE titanic_data.passengers_adults_46_60
PARTITION OF titanic_data.passengers_partitioned

FOR VALUES FROM (46) TO (60);
```

Move Data to the New Partitions

Now, we need to move the data from the **passengers_adults** partition to the newly created partitions:

```
INSERT INTO titanic_data.passengers_adults_18_30

SELECT * FROM titanic_data.passengers_adults WHERE age
BETWEEN 18 AND 30;


INSERT INTO titanic_data.passengers_adults_31_45

SELECT * FROM titanic_data.passengers_adults WHERE age
BETWEEN 31 AND 45;
```

```
INSERT INTO titanic_data.passengers_adults_46_60
SELECT * FROM titanic_data.passengers_adults WHERE age
BETWEEN 46 AND 60;
```

Drop the Old Partition

Once the data has been moved, we can drop the original **passengers_adults** partition:

```
DROP TABLE titanic_data.passengers_adults;
```

Verify the New Partitions

You can now verify that the new partitions are in place and that the data has been properly distributed:

```
SELECT * FROM titanic_data.passengers_partitioned WHERE
age BETWEEN 18 AND 60;
```

This query will now access the appropriate sub-partitions (**passengers_adults_18_30**, **passengers_adults_31_45**, **passengers_adults_46_60**), improving performance for age-based queries.

PostgreSQL 17's enhanced partition management features make it easier to dynamically adjust partitions, offering greater flexibility and control over large datasets like the Titanic dataset. This allows you to maintain high performance and keep the database well-organized as it scales.

Optimizing Queries on Partitioned Tables

It is known that optimizing queries on partitioned tables requires more than just partitioning the data, as it requires understanding **partition pruning** and employing the right **indexing strategies**. Partition pruning ensures that only relevant partitions are scanned during query execution, reducing the overhead and improving query efficiency. Meanwhile, indexing ensures that queries accessing individual partitions can still benefit from rapid data retrieval.

So here now, we will explore how partition pruning works and how to set up indexes on partitioned tables, using the partitioned Titanic dataset we previously created.

Sample Program: Partition Pruning in Range Partitioning

Partition pruning is the process by which PostgreSQL eliminates irrelevant partitions from a query before scanning. When a query involves filtering based on the partitioning key, PostgreSQL identifies the partitions that contain the relevant data and skips the others, significantly reducing query execution time.

Here, we consider the Titanic dataset, where we partitioned the **passengers_partitioned** table by age ranges (children, adults, and seniors). Suppose we want to run a query that retrieves only adult passengers (ages 18-60).

Query Without Partition Pruning

Without partition pruning, PostgreSQL would have to scan all partitions to retrieve the data, including those that don't contain relevant information. This is inefficient, particularly when only one or two partitions contain the necessary data.

Given below is a query that selects adult passengers:

```
SELECT * FROM titanic_data.passengers_partitioned WHERE
age BETWEEN 18 AND 60;
```

Partition Pruning in Action

When PostgreSQL executes this query, it uses partition pruning to identify that only the **passengers_adults** partition contains data for ages between 18 and 60. As a result, PostgreSQL will prune the **passengers_children** and **passengers_seniors** partitions and scan only the **passengers_adults** partition.

You can see partition pruning in action by using the **EXPLAIN** command to view the query execution plan:

```
EXPLAIN SELECT * FROM titanic_data.passengers_partitioned
WHERE age BETWEEN 18 AND 60;
```

The output will show that only the relevant partition (**passengers_adults**) is being scanned, reducing the overall execution time.

Automatic Partition Pruning

PostgreSQL handles partition pruning automatically whenever the query condition involves the partition key. However, for partition pruning to work effectively, it's essential to write queries that take advantage of the partitioning structure.

For example, the filtering condition (**WHERE age BETWEEN 18 AND 60**) directly corresponds to the partition key must be ensured.

Sample Program: Indexing Range-Partitioned Tables

While partition pruning optimizes which partitions get scanned, indexing ensures that queries within each partition can be executed efficiently. When a partitioned table grows large, using the right indexing strategy can greatly improve performance, especially for queries that do not directly involve the partition key.

For the Titanic dataset partitioned by age, we can further optimize queries by adding indexes to the partitions. We will assume we frequently query passengers based on their **name** or **ticket class** in addition to age.

Creating Indexes on Partitions

Instead of creating a single index for the entire table, we create separate indexes on each partition. For example, to improve searches by **name** within the **passengers_adults** partition, we can create an index on the **name** column:

```
CREATE INDEX idx_adults_name ON
titanic_data.passengers_adults (name);
```

Similarly, we can create indexes on the **name** column for other partitions:

```
CREATE INDEX idx_children_name ON
titanic_data.passengers_children (name);

CREATE INDEX idx_seniors_name ON
titanic_data.passengers_seniors (name);
```

These indexes ensure that even within a partition, searches by passenger name will be faster.

Querying with Indexed Partitions

Now, we run a query to find all adult passengers named "John Doe." PostgreSQL will first use partition pruning to scan only the **passengers_adults** partition and then use the index on **name** to quickly retrieve the matching rows:

```
SELECT * FROM titanic_data.passengers_partitioned WHERE
name = 'John Doe' AND age BETWEEN 18 AND 60;
```

This combination of partition pruning and indexing ensures that the query is executed efficiently, scanning only the relevant partition and using the index to speed up the search.

Sample Program: Indexing List-Partitioned Tables

For the Titanic dataset partitioned by **ticket class** (First-Class, Second-Class, Third-Class), we can similarly create indexes on commonly queried fields, such as **ticket price** or **survival status**.

Creating Indexes on Partitions

We will create indexes on the **`details -> 'ticket' ->> 'price'`** field, which stores ticket prices in the JSONB **`details`** column. We can create a GIN index to optimize queries that involve searching or filtering by ticket price:

```
CREATE INDEX idx_first_class_ticket_price ON
titanic_data.passengers_first_class USING GIN ((details -
> 'ticket' ->> 'price'));
```

We repeat this process for other partitions:

```
CREATE INDEX idx_second_class_ticket_price ON
titanic_data.passengers_second_class USING GIN ((details
-> 'ticket' ->> 'price'));

CREATE INDEX idx_third_class_ticket_price ON
titanic_data.passengers_third_class USING GIN ((details -
> 'ticket' ->> 'price'));
```

Querying with Indexed Partitions

To query for all **First-Class passengers** who paid more than $150 for their ticket:

```
SELECT * FROM titanic_data.passengers_by_class WHERE
(details -> 'ticket' ->> 'price')::NUMERIC > 150 AND
details ->> 'ticket' ->> 'type' = 'First-Class';
```

This query will use partition pruning to scan only the **`passengers_first_class`** partition and leverage the GIN index on ticket prices to optimize the search within that partition.

Sample Program: Indexing Hash-Partitioned Tables

In hash partitioning, data is distributed evenly across partitions based on a hash function. For example, in our Titanic dataset partitioned by **passenger ID**, we can create indexes on the **id** column or other frequently queried columns such as **gender** or **survived**.

Creating Indexes on Hash Partitions

We will create indexes on the **gender** column across all hash partitions to optimize queries that filter passengers by gender:

```
CREATE INDEX idx_hash_0_gender ON
titanic_data.passengers_hash_0 (gender);

CREATE INDEX idx_hash_1_gender ON
titanic_data.passengers_hash_1 (gender);

CREATE INDEX idx_hash_2_gender ON
titanic_data.passengers_hash_2 (gender);

CREATE INDEX idx_hash_3_gender ON
titanic_data.passengers_hash_3 (gender);
```

This ensures that queries involving the **gender** field will be optimized, regardless of which partition the data resides in.

Querying with Indexed Hash Partitions

When querying for female passengers with a specific **id**, PostgreSQL will use partition pruning to narrow down the relevant partition (based on the hash of the **id**), and then use the index on **gender** to optimize the search:

```
SELECT * FROM titanic_data.passengers_hash_partitioned
WHERE id = 3 AND gender = 'female';
```

This query benefits from both partition pruning (to narrow down to the relevant hash partition) and indexing (to quickly retrieve rows within that partition).

Monitoring Query Performance

PostgreSQL provides several tools for analyzing query execution.

Using EXPLAIN ANALYZE

The **EXPLAIN ANALYZE** command allows you to see the execution plan for a query, including whether partition pruning and indexes are being used. For example:

```
EXPLAIN ANALYZE SELECT * FROM
titanic_data.passengers_partitioned WHERE age BETWEEN 18
AND 60;
```

The output will show if partition pruning occurred and which indexes were used in the query.

Monitoring Index Usage

The **pg_stat_user_indexes** view provides statistics on how often each index is used. This can help you determine whether your indexes are being utilized efficiently:

```
SELECT indexrelname, idx_scan, idx_tup_read,
idx_tup_fetch

FROM pg_stat_user_indexes

WHERE relname = 'passengers_partitioned';
```

Low **idx_scan** values might indicate that certain indexes are underutilized and could be candidates for optimization or removal.

By combining **partition pruning** with an appropriate **indexing strategy**, PostgreSQL can significantly improve query performance on partitioned tables. Partition pruning ensures that only relevant partitions are scanned, while indexes within each partition speed up data retrieval.

Summary

To conclude, we demonstrated the most efficient methods for managing large datasets by implementing and optimizing table partitioning strategies in PostgreSQL. We started by getting to grips with the different types of partitioning, including range, list, and hash partitioning, and how they can be used. We partitioned the Titanic dataset to organize data into smaller, more manageable partitions based on passenger age, ticket class, and ID.

We learned how to add, merge, and split partitions as the dataset evolved. The chapter ended with a clear explanation of how to optimize queries on partitioned tables using partition pruning and indexing strategies. We also implemented specific indexes on individual partitions, which optimized query execution by ensuring rapid data retrieval within each partition. These strategies significantly improved the performance of complex queries on large datasets, ensuring the database remained responsive as it scaled.

Chapter 7: Backup and Recovery Best Practices

Brief Overview

This chapter focuses on creating a dependable backup and recovery strategy. We start by learning how to create an effective backup strategy, which includes assessing system requirements like recovery time objectives (RTO) and recovery point objectives (RPO). We then examine physical backups with pg_basebackup, a tool that generates consistent physical snapshots of the database cluster.

Next, we'll look at logical backups using pg_dump and pg_restore, which give you more precise control over backup and restore operations. These tools are useful for backing up specific schemas or tables, giving you more flexibility with data management. Finally, we introduce BART (Backup and Recovery Tool), to automate backup and recovery processes, including incremental backups, and streamlines the entire workflow, particularly for large-scale deployments. Put together, these topics cover all you need to know about backup methodologies to keep your data safe and get back up and running quickly after a disaster.

Designing a Backup Strategy

Two critical metrics that influence the design of any backup strategy are **RPO** and **RTO**. Once these objectives are assessed, the choice between **physical backups** (which replicate the entire database) and **logical backups** (which allow for selective, schema-specific backups) becomes clearer.

Before deciding on a backup strategy, it's important to assess your business needs by determining the RPO and RTO. These metrics help you understand the acceptable amount of data loss and the time needed to restore operations after a failure.

RPO

RPO measures the maximum acceptable amount of data loss in the event of a disaster. For example, if your database experiences a failure, RPO indicates how far back in time you can afford to recover without severely impacting operations. A low RPO means your system must capture data frequently (such as in real-time or with frequent backups), while a higher RPO means you can tolerate losing several minutes or hours of data.

For instance:

- **High RPO**: If you can tolerate losing up to a day's worth of data, daily backups might suffice. This is common for systems that don't see constant data changes.
- **Low RPO**: For high-transaction systems, like e-commerce platforms or financial services, where any data loss is unacceptable, you would need continuous backups, possibly using **streaming replication** or **point-in-time recovery (PITR)**.

RTO

RTO defines how quickly your system needs to be restored to a functioning state after a failure. A low RTO requires a more efficient and fast recovery method, while a higher RTO allows for more flexibility in the recovery process.

For example:

- **Low RTO**: If your system needs to be back online within minutes, then you will need a robust strategy, such as having a hot standby or using tools like **pg_basebackup** for physical backups, which offer faster restore times.
- **High RTO**: If your system can tolerate several hours of downtime, you can afford a slower recovery process, such as using logical backups, which take longer to restore but offer flexibility in restoring specific parts of the database.

Based on your RPO and RTO assessments, you will need to choose between **physical backups** and **logical backups**. Each type has its advantages and is suited to different scenarios.

Sample Program: Using `pg_basebackup` for Physical Backups

Physical Backup Overview

Physical backups involve copying the database cluster's entire data directory. This type of backup is ideal when you need to back up the entire database quickly and efficiently. Physical backups are often faster to restore because they copy the data at the block level, and they preserve the entire database state, including system catalogs and WAL (Write-Ahead Logging) files.

Physical backups are typically used in conjunction with **WAL archiving** and **PITR**. This means the system continuously records changes, and the backups can restore the database to any specific point in time, minimizing data loss (low RPO). Restoring from a physical backup can be faster because it doesn't involve re-creating the database objects. Instead, it restores the entire cluster at once, leading to lower recovery times (low RTO).

When to Choose Physical Backups?

- When you need **fast recovery times** (low RTO).
- When your database contains **large volumes of data**.
- When you require **point-in-time recovery** with minimal data loss (low RPO).
- When you want to back up the entire database cluster, including all databases and configuration files.

Using 'Pg_basebackup'

pg_basebackup is the standard tool for creating physical backups in PostgreSQL. It replicates the entire database cluster and is often used with replication or high-availability configurations.

Given below is how you can use **pg_basebackup** to create a physical backup:

```
pg_basebackup -D /path/to/backup/dir -F tar -z -X fetch -
P
```

Here,

- **-D**: Specifies the directory to store the backup.
- **-F tar**: Creates the backup in the tar format.
- **-z**: Compresses the backup.
- **-X fetch**: Ensures that all WAL files are included.
- **-P**: Shows progress while the backup is being created.

The physical backup created with **pg_basebackup** can be restored by simply unpacking the archive and placing it in the appropriate directory.

Sample Program: Using `pg_dump` and `pg_restore` for Logical Backups

Logical Backups Overview

Logical backups, in contrast, involve exporting database objects like tables, schemas, and roles. These backups are created using tools such as **pg_dump** and **pg_restore**. Logical backups offer greater flexibility because they allow you to back up specific parts of the database (e.g., individual schemas or tables) and can be used to migrate data between different versions of PostgreSQL.

- **RPO considerations**: Logical backups are generally less frequent than physical backups because they take longer to create. Thus, they might not be suitable for low RPO requirements unless combined with other mechanisms like WAL archiving.
- **RTO considerations**: Restoring from a logical backup is slower because PostgreSQL needs to recreate all database objects and repopulate data from scratch, leading to higher recovery times (high RTO).

When to Choose Logical Backups?

- When you need **flexibility** in backup and recovery, such as restoring only certain tables or schemas.

- When you are **migrating data** between different PostgreSQL versions or instances.
- When you need **individual table-level** backups for targeted recovery or auditing purposes.
- When RTO is less critical, and the backup size is manageable.

Using 'pg_dump' and 'pg_restore'

pg_dump is the standard tool for creating logical backups. It generates SQL scripts that can recreate database objects and data.

Given below is how to back up the **Titanic** database using **pg_dump**:

```
pg_dump -U postgres -d titanic_db -F c -f
/path/to/backup/titanic_db.backup
```

Here, **-F c** creates the backup in a custom format, which is useful for restoration with **pg_restore**.

Now, to restore the backup using **pg_restore**:

```
pg_restore -U postgres -d titanic_db_restored
/path/to/backup/titanic_db.backup
```

This restores the entire Titanic database, including its tables, schemas, and data.

In many cases, the best strategy is to use a combination of both physical and logical backups, leveraging the strengths of each. A common strategy might involve taking a **weekly physical backup** and performing **daily logical backups** of critical tables or schemas. This approach ensures that the entire database can be restored quickly if needed, while also offering the flexibility to restore specific parts of the database if only a portion of the data is corrupted.

Physical Backups with pg_basebackup

pg_basebackup is a built-in PostgreSQL utility specifically designed for creating **physical backups** of an entire PostgreSQL cluster. It copies the entire data directory, including all configurations, table data, and write-ahead logs, enabling easy restoration in the event of a failure.

Here, we will learn to create **consistent physical backups** using pg_basebackup, stream these backups for large databases, and handle large datasets efficiently.

Consistent Backups with pg_basebackup

The goal of a physical backup is to create an exact copy of the database cluster that can be restored quickly and accurately. **pg_basebackup** ensures consistency by including **Write-Ahead Logs**, which record every transaction that has occurred. This ensures that the database can be restored to a consistent state.

Basic Backup Command

To create a consistent physical backup, the most basic usage of **pg_basebackup** is as follows:

```
pg_basebackup -D /path/to/backup/dir -F tar -z -X fetch -
P
```

Here,

- **`-D /path/to/backup/dir`**: Specifies the directory where the backup should be stored.
- **`-F tar`**: Creates the backup in **tar** format, making it easier to move or compress the backup files.
- **`-z`**: Compresses the backup to save disk space.
- **`-X fetch`**: Ensures that all WAL files are fetched at the end of the backup, guaranteeing consistency.
- **`-P`**: Displays progress as the backup is being created.

For example, to back up the Titanic database cluster, you would specify the location where the backup should be stored:

```
pg_basebackup -D /backups/titanic_cluster_backup -F tar -
z -X fetch -P
```

Consistency with WAL files

WAL files are essential for replaying the changes made during the backup process and bringing the restored database to a consistent state. Without these files, a backup may be inconsistent, especially in a busy database with active writes during the backup.

By using **`-X fetch`**, PostgreSQL automatically fetches the required WAL files at the end of the backup, ensuring that the database will be consistent upon restoration. Alternatively, you can use **`-X stream`** to stream the WAL files in real time, which will be learned in the next section.

Verifying the Backup

Once the backup is complete, it's essential to verify that the backup directory contains both the **data directory** and **WAL files**. This ensures the integrity of the backup and prepares it for restoration.

To check the contents of the backup:

```
ls /backups/titanic_cluster_backup/
```

You should see the **data files** and **WAL archive**. These files guarantee that the database can be restored to its last consistent state.

Streaming Backups for Large Databases

Streaming is particularly useful in high-availability (HA) environments, where the goal is to have continuous backups without overloading the primary server or taking snapshots that are too large to manage in a single operation. Streaming backups allow you to manage large datasets by continuously sending both data files and WAL segments in real time to an external location, such as a standby server or remote storage.

Streaming WAL files

The **-X stream** option in **pg_basebackup** allows for real-time streaming of **WAL segments** during the backup process. This is particularly beneficial for large databases, as it streams the WAL files in real time rather than fetching them at the end of the backup. Streaming reduces the I/O overhead on the primary server and allows backups to be made without pausing database operations.

```
pg_basebackup -D /backups/streamed_backup -F tar -z -X
stream -P
```

This command will:

- Stream the backup data as well as the WAL files in real-time.
- Compress the files to save disk space.
- Ensure that you get a complete, consistent backup even in a high-transaction environment.

Handling Large Databases during Backup

For large PostgreSQL databases, managing backup size and time becomes critical. Some best practices for handling large databases during backup include:

- Compression

Use the **-z** option to compress the backup files, which reduces the disk space required. For extremely large databases, you can further reduce the size by specifying a compression level.

```
pg_basebackup -D /backups/streamed_backup -F tar -z5 -X
stream -P
```

This sets the compression level to **5**, which offers a balance between compression speed and size.

- Parallelization

Use multiple worker threads to speed up the backup process for very large databases. The **-j** option enables parallelism, with the number of threads specified as an argument:

```
pg_basebackup -D /backups/titanic_large_backup -F tar -z
-X stream -j 4 -P
```

In the above, **-j 4** creates the backup using four parallel worker threads, reducing the total time taken to perform the backup.

- Storage Management

When backing up large datasets, ensure that the destination storage has enough space to handle both the raw data and the WAL files. Regularly monitor disk usage and implement automatic archival or cleanup scripts to manage older backups.

Handling Backups for Large Databases

When working with large databases, it's essential to handle backups efficiently. In addition to the techniques mentioned above, there are additional strategies to ensure that backups do not negatively impact the performance of your production database.

Continuous Archiving and WAL Segments

For large databases with frequent updates, it's recommended to enable **WAL archiving** to continuously stream changes. This helps reduce the size of each individual backup and enables **PITR**.

To enable continuous WAL archiving, modify the **postgresql.conf** file:

```
archive_mode = on
```

```
archive_command = 'cp %p /backups/wal_archive/%f'
```

This ensures that each WAL segment is archived to a separate directory as soon as it is created. When restoring a backup, you can use these WAL segments to replay the changes and bring the database to the desired state.

Replication Slots for Streaming

Replication slots help ensure that the primary server retains all necessary WAL segments for a standby server or backup system. This prevents WAL files from being recycled or deleted before they can be backed up.

To create a replication slot for streaming backups:

```
psql -c "SELECT * FROM
pg_create_physical_replication_slot('backup_slot');"
```

Then, you can use this replication slot during backup to ensure that no WAL data is lost:

```
pg_basebackup -D /backups/titanic_streamed_backup -F tar
-X stream --slot=backup_slot -P
```

Backing up to Remote Location

To prevent backups from using local disk space, you can stream backups directly to a **remote server** over SSH or another protocol. You can stream backups to a remote server using tools like **rsync** or directly over SSH as shown below:

```
pg_basebackup -D - -F tar -z -X stream -P | ssh
user@backupserver "cat > /backups/streamed_backup.tar.gz"
```

This command streams the backup directly to the remote server, where it is compressed and stored.

When dealing with large PostgreSQL databases, streaming WAL files, using parallel workers, and managing storage efficiently are essential for reducing the backup time and size. Techniques like replication slots, continuous archiving, and remote backups can handle large datasets effectively and your database is always protected and can be restored quickly.

Logical Backups with pg_dump and pg_restore

In this section, we will perform **selective backups** of individual schemas and tables using **`pg_dump`** and how to restore these backups with **`pg_restore`**.

Backing up Individual Schemas and Tables

Logical backups allow you to back up specific parts of your database rather than the entire cluster. This is particularly useful when managing large datasets where full backups may be unnecessary, or when you need to migrate a portion of the database.

Backing up a Specific Schema

Here, we back up the **public** schema in the Titanic database, which contains the **passengers** table. To back up a single schema, use the **-n** option in **pg_dump**.

```
pg_dump -U postgres -d titanic_db -n public -F c -f
/backups/titanic_public_schema.backup
```

In the above script,

- **`-n public`**: Specifies the **public** schema to back up.
- **`-F c`**: Creates the backup in a **custom format**, which can be restored using **`pg_restore`**.
- **`-f /backups/titanic_public_schema.backup`**: Specifies the output file where the backup will be saved.

This command will back up all the objects within the public schema, including tables, indexes, and sequences, but won't include data from other schemas (if they exist).

Backing up a Specific Table

To back up an individual table, such as the **passengers** table, you can use the **-t** option in **pg_dump**. This allows you to back up just one table and its associated data.

```
pg_dump -U postgres -d titanic_db -t passengers -F c -f
/backups/titanic_passengers_table.backup
```

Here,

- **`-t passengers`**: Specifies the **passengers** table to back up.

- **`-F c`**: Creates the backup in a **custom format**, which allows for flexible restoration.
- **`-f /backups/titanic_passengers_table.backup`**: Specifies the output file for the backup.

This command backs up the structure and data of the **passengers** table but doesn't include other tables or objects within the database.

Backing up Multiple Tables

You can also back up multiple tables by specifying more than one **-t** option. For example, if the Titanic database had multiple tables such as **passengers** and **tickets**, and we wanted to back up both, we would run:

```
pg_dump -U postgres -d titanic_db -t passengers -t
tickets -F c -f /backups/titanic_selected_tables.backup
```

This will create a backup containing only the **passengers** and **tickets** tables, excluding other tables in the database.

Restoring Backups with pg_restore

The logical backups created with **pg_dump** can be restored using the **pg_restore** tool. Depending on the backup format, **pg_restore** allows for selective restoration of specific tables, schemas, or even data, making it a versatile tool for managing backups.

Restoring a Specific Schema

To restore the **public** schema from the backup we created earlier, use the following command:

```
pg_restore -U postgres -d titanic_db_restored -n public
/backups/titanic_public_schema.backup
```

Here,

- **`-n public`**: Specifies that we want to restore only the **public** schema.
- **`titanic_db_restored`**: The target database where the schema will be restored.
- **`/backups/titanic_public_schema.backup`**: The backup file from which the schema will be restored.

This restores the entire **public** schema, including all tables, sequences, and indexes within that schema.

Restoring a Specific Table

To restore the **passengers** table, which we backed up individually, use the following command:

```
pg_restore -U postgres -d titanic_db_restored -t
passengers /backups/titanic_passengers_table.backup
```

Here,

- **`-t passengers`**: Specifies the **passengers** table to be restored.
- **`titanic_db_restored`**: The target database where the table will be restored.
- **`/backups/titanic_passengers_table.backup`**: The backup file containing the table data and structure.

This command restores the **passengers** table, including its data and structure, to the specified database.

Selective Restore from Full Backup

If you created a full database backup but want to restore only certain parts, **pg_restore** allows you to select specific objects to restore. For example, if you have a full backup of the Titanic database but only want to restore the **tickets** table, you would run:

```
pg_restore -U postgres -d titanic_db_restored -t tickets
/backups/titanic_full_backup.backup
```

This restores only the **tickets** table from a full backup file, excluding all other tables and objects.

Overwriting Existing Data

When restoring data into an existing database, the default behavior of **`pg_restore`** is to append the data to existing tables. If you want to replace the existing data, you can use the **`--clean`** option, which drops the existing objects before restoring them.

For example, to overwrite the existing **`passengers`** table with data from the backup:

```
pg_restore -U postgres -d titanic_db_restored -t
passengers --clean
/backups/titanic_passengers_table.backup
```

This command drops the existing **passengers** table and recreates it from the backup, ensuring that the restored data doesn't conflict with any pre-existing data.

Whether you are backing up specific schemas, individual tables, or creating full database backups, the ability to selectively restore parts of the database makes **pg_dump** the goto tool for database administrators.

Introducing BART

BART (Backup and Recovery Tool) is an enterprise-grade backup solution designed for PostgreSQL that simplifies the process of creating, managing, and restoring backups. BART automates and streamlines both **physical backups** and **PITR**, making it easier to manage backups for large databases or complex systems.

Unlike traditional tools like **`pg_basebackup`** and **`pg_dump`**, BART offers advanced features such as **incremental backups**, **WAL file archiving**, and **backup scheduling**. These features provide more efficient storage management and faster recovery times, especially for high-availability PostgreSQL systems.

Key Features of BART

BART stands out from other PostgreSQL backup tools due to its powerful automation and management features, making it suitable for enterprises handling large databases or multiple PostgreSQL instances.

- Full backups

BART performs a full physical backup of your PostgreSQL database cluster, much like **`pg_basebackup`**. This includes all necessary data files and configurations required to restore the entire database.

- Incremental backups

BART offers the ability to create incremental backups, which only back up the changes made since the last full or incremental backup. This reduces storage space requirements and speeds up the backup process.

- WAL Archiving

BART automatically archives Write-Ahead Log files to ensure that no transaction data is lost, enabling PITR. This is especially useful for high-transaction databases where every write operation needs to be recoverable.

- Backup Automation and Scheduling

BART allows you to schedule backups, ensuring regular and automated database backups without manual intervention. It also helps manage backup retention policies, automatically purging older backups according to your set rules.

- PITR

BART supports **PITR**, which allows you to restore your database to a specific point in time, using both full backups and the WAL logs that BART archives. This feature is essential for recovering from data corruption or accidental data loss.

- Backup Integrity Verification

BART provides backup validation, ensuring that backups are consistent and can be restored. It checks the integrity of both data files and WAL segments, providing added reliability in disaster recovery scenarios.

Installing BART

To start using BART, you first need to install it on your PostgreSQL server. The installation process requires downloading the BART package, configuring it for your PostgreSQL cluster, and ensuring it has the appropriate permissions to manage backups and WAL files.

Now, before you install it, ensure you have the following:

- PostgreSQL 9.6 or higher (BART is designed for modern PostgreSQL versions).
- Access to the PostgreSQL server and its configuration files.
- Sufficient storage for backups and archived WAL logs.
- An archive directory where BART can store backup files and WAL segments.

Installing BART

- Download the BART Package

Visit the EnterpriseDB repository to download the BART package:

```
wget https://download.enterprisedb.com/postgresql/edb-bart-<version>.tar.gz
```

Replace **`<version>`** with the latest version of BART.

- Extract the Package

```
tar -xzf edb-bart-<version>.tar.gz
```

- Install BART

Navigate to the extracted directory and run the installation commands:

```
cd edb-bart-<version>

./configure

make

sudo make install
```

- Verify Installation

To confirm that BART has been installed, run the following command:

```
bart --version
```

You should see the version of BART that was installed.

Configuring BART

After installation, BART needs to be configured to work with your PostgreSQL database cluster. The main configuration file for BART is **bart.cfg**, which specifies where backups should be stored and how WAL archiving is handled.

- Edit the Configuration file

Open the **bart.cfg** file in a text editor:

```
nano /etc/bart.cfg
```

- Specify the Archive Directory

Set the location for backups and WAL file archives:

```
[BART]

backup_path = /backups/bart_backups

wal_path = /backups/bart_wal_archive

Configure the PostgreSQL Instance
```

Under the **[PostgreSQL]** section, provide the details for your PostgreSQL server:

```
[PostgreSQL]

host = localhost

port = 5432

user = postgres
```

- Enable WAL Archiving in PostgreSQL

To enable WAL archiving, update the **postgresql.conf** file:

```
archive_mode = on

archive_command = 'cp %p /backups/bart_wal_archive/%f'
```

This command archives WAL files to the directory where BART can manage them.

Automating Backups and Restores with BART

Once BART is installed and configured, you can start using it to automate backups and restores. This section demonstrates how to create full and incremental backups, schedule them, and restore the database when needed.

Creating Full Backups

To create a full backup of your PostgreSQL database cluster, use the **backup** command:

```
bart backup --pgdata /var/lib/postgresql/data --backup-
label "full_backup_2024"
```

Here,

- **--pgdata**: The path to your PostgreSQL data directory.
- **--backup-label**: A label to identify the backup.

This command creates a full backup and stores it in the backup path specified in **bart.cfg**. You can check the backup status with the following command:

```
bart show-backups
```

Creating Incremental Backups

After performing a full backup, you can use BART to create incremental backups. These only store the changes made since the last full or incremental backup, saving both time and storage space.

For example, to create an incremental backup:

```
bart backup --pgdata /var/lib/postgresql/data --backup-
label "incremental_backup_2024" --incremental
```

This command ensures that only the differences from the last backup are recorded.

Automating Backups with Scheduling

To automate backups, you can use **cron jobs** to schedule full and incremental backups at regular intervals. For example, to schedule a full backup every Sunday at 2 AM, add the following line to your crontab:

```
0 2 * * 0 /usr/bin/bart backup --pgdata
/var/lib/postgresql/data --backup-label
"weekly_full_backup"
```

Similarly, to schedule daily incremental backups at 2 AM:

```
0 2 * * 1-6 /usr/bin/bart backup --pgdata
/var/lib/postgresql/data --backup-label
"daily_incremental_backup" --incremental
```

These scheduled jobs ensure that backups are created regularly without manual intervention.

Restoring a Full Backup

To restore a database from a full backup, use the following command:

```
bart restore --pgdata /var/lib/postgresql/data --backup-
id <backup-id>
```

Here, replace **<backup-id>** with the identifier of the backup you want to restore, which can be found using the **bart show-backups** command.

BART simplifies and automates backup and recovery tasks for PostgreSQL by offering full and incremental backups, automated scheduling, and point-in-time recovery. By automating backups using BART, administrators can maintain data integrity and ensure rapid recovery with minimal manual effort. For large PostgreSQL clusters, the use of BART ensures that both storage space and recovery times are optimized for enterprise environments.

Summary

Collectively, we have learned the PostgreSQL database backup and recovery strategies. First, we learned how to create an effective backup strategy using the RPO and RTO. Next, we looked into physical backups with pg_basebackup, which allowed us to create consistent full database backups by copying the entire PostgreSQL data directory. We also practiced streaming these backups in real time to better manage large datasets. This section discussed how to optimize backups of large databases using techniques like compression and parallelism.

We then learned how to perform logical backups with pg_dump and pg_restore. This method is ideal for performing partial restores and migrations between PostgreSQL versions. Finally, we learned how BART can automate backups, including incremental backups.

CHAPTER 8: STREAMING REPLICATION AND HIGH AVAILABILITY

Brief Overview

This chapter teaches you how to implement robust high availability solutions that ensure continuous access to your PostgreSQL databases despite hardware or software failures. First, we'll look at the key aspects of streaming replication and high availability. Then, we will perform setting up streaming replication, which teaches us how to configure a primary (master) server and one or more standby (replica) servers to replicate data in real time.

The next step is to manage replication, which includes monitoring replication status, adjusting configurations for performance, and resolving replication delays or conflicts. The final topic, failover and switchover, walks us through the scenarios in which the primary server fails. We also look at how to change roles across servers for maintenance or load balancing purposes.

Setting up Streaming Replication

Streaming replication in PostgreSQL enables real-time data replication from a **primary** (master) server to one or more **standby** (replica) servers. This process is vital for **high availability** and **disaster recovery**, ensuring that the database remains available even if the primary server fails. Before diving into the setup, it's important to understand the two main types of replication in PostgreSQL—**physical** and **logical** replication—as well as the differences between **synchronous** and **asynchronous** replication modes.

Physical vs. Logical Replication

Replication in PostgreSQL comes in two forms: **physical** and **logical**. Understanding the differences between them helps you choose the best method for your use case.

Physical Replication

Physical replication operates at the **block level** and replicates the entire state of the database cluster. It copies the **WAL (Write-Ahead Logging)** files from the primary server to the standby server, allowing the standby server to replay those changes and maintain an exact copy of the primary. It is simple, efficient, and captures the entire database state, including system catalogs, indexes, and data. The replica is **read-only**, and it cannot be used to perform additional write operations or to contain a different database structure than the primary.

Logical Replication

Logical replication works at the **table or database level**. It replicates changes to individual tables (such as **INSERT**, **UPDATE**, and **DELETE** operations) rather than at the block level. Logical replication allows for more flexibility, including replicating between different versions of PostgreSQL or between different database structures. Replicas can be used for both **read** and **write** operations on different tables. It allows you to replicate specific tables or databases rather than the entire cluster. It has more overhead than physical replication and can be more complex to set up and manage.

Synchronous vs. Asynchronous

When setting up streaming replication, you can choose between **synchronous** and **asynchronous** replication modes. The key difference between these modes lies in how they handle data consistency between the primary and standby servers.

Asynchronous Replication

Asynchronous replication is the default and most common mode in PostgreSQL. In this mode, the primary server does not wait for the standby server to acknowledge that it has received the changes. Once the changes are written to the WAL on the primary server, the primary continues to operate without waiting for the standby. It offers better performance because the primary server doesn't need to wait for the standby to acknowledge every transaction. There's a potential for **data loss** because, in the event of a failure, the most recent changes might not have been replicated to the standby server.

Synchronous Replication

In synchronous replication, the primary server waits for confirmation from the standby server before committing the transaction. This ensures that no data is lost in case of failure, as the standby always has an up-to-date copy of the data. It guarantees that all transactions are safely stored on both the primary and standby, ensuring zero data loss in the event of failure. This mode introduces **latency**, as the primary server must wait for the standby to acknowledge each transaction, potentially slowing down the system.

Configuring Streaming Replication

Now that we've covered the basic concepts, we can proceed to configure **streaming replication**. In this demonstration, we will set up **physical streaming replication** using **asynchronous mode** (though switching to synchronous is possible with minor changes).

System Setup

To understand the replication, we will configure two servers:

- **Primary server** (192.168.1.10)
- **Standby server** (192.168.1.11)

We will also use **replication slots** to ensure that the primary retains the WAL files that the standby needs, even if the standby is temporarily disconnected.

Configure Primary Server

- Edit postgresql.conf

On the primary server, we need to enable replication settings in **postgresql.conf**.

```
sudo nano /etc/postgresql/13/main/postgresql.conf
```

Make the following changes:

```
listen_addresses = 'localhost,192.168.1.10'  # Listen on
the server's IP

wal_level = replica                          # Enable WAL
for replication

max_wal_senders = 5                          # Number of
replication connections

wal_keep_size = 64MB                         # Retain WAL
segments for replication

archive_mode = on                            # Enable WAL
archiving

archive_command = 'cp %p
/var/lib/postgresql/wal_archive/%f'
```

These settings ensure that the primary server allows replication connections and stores enough WAL files to maintain the replica's consistency.

- Edit pg_hba.conf

The **pg_hba.conf** file controls access to the PostgreSQL cluster. To allow replication connections, add the following entry:

```
sudo nano /etc/postgresql/13/main/pg_hba.conf
```

Add the following line to grant replication access to the standby server's IP:

```
host    replication    all             192.168.1.11/32
md5
```

This entry ensures that the standby server can connect to the primary for replication purposes.

- Create a Replication User

You'll need to create a user on the primary server that will be used for replication:

```
CREATE USER rep_user WITH REPLICATION ENCRYPTED PASSWORD
'rep_password';
```

- Create a Replication Slot

Replication slots ensure that the primary retains the necessary WAL files until they are replicated, preventing data loss if the standby is temporarily disconnected. Create a replication slot on the primary server:

```
SELECT * FROM
pg_create_physical_replication_slot('standby_slot');
```

This command creates a **physical replication slot** named **standby_slot**.

- Restart PostgreSQL

After making these changes, restart the PostgreSQL service on the primary server:

```
sudo systemctl restart postgresql
```

Configure Standby Server

Next, we will configure the standby server to connect to the primary and start receiving replicated data.

- Stop PostgreSQL on the Standby

First, stop the PostgreSQL service on the standby server:

```
sudo systemctl stop postgresql
```

- Copy the Data Directory from the Primary

To create a consistent starting point for replication, we need to copy the data directory from the primary server to the standby. Use **pg_basebackup** to copy the data directory:

```
pg_basebackup -h 192.168.1.10 -D
/var/lib/postgresql/13/main -U rep_user -P --wal-
method=stream --slot=standby_slot
```

Here,

- **-h**: Specifies the IP of the primary server.
- **-D**: Specifies the data directory on the standby.
- **-U**: Uses the replication user created earlier.
- **--wal-method=stream**: Streams the WAL files while copying the data.
- **--slot=standby_slot**: Uses the replication slot created earlier to maintain WAL file consistency.

- Edit postgresql.conf

After copying the data directory, configure the standby server by modifying **postgresql.conf**:

```
sudo nano /etc/postgresql/13/main/postgresql.conf
```

Add or modify the following settings:

```
hot_standby = on                              # Enable read
queries on standby

primary_conninfo = 'host=192.168.1.10 port=5432
user=rep_user password=rep_password'

primary_slot_name = 'standby_slot'            # Use the
replication slot
```

These settings ensure the standby server connects to the primary and uses the correct replication slot for consistent data transfer.

Finally, start the PostgreSQL service on the standby server:

```
sudo systemctl start postgresql
```

The standby server will now connect to the primary server and begin replicating data in real-time.

Verifying Streaming Replication

You can verify that streaming replication is working by checking the replication status on the primary server.

For this, run the following query:

```
SELECT * FROM pg_stat_replication;
```

This query will show details of the connected standby servers, including the state of replication and the lag between the primary and standby.

These steps set up **streaming replication** between a primary and a standby PostgreSQL server using **physical replication** and **asynchronous mode**. Here, we also ensured data consistency with **replication slots**, guaranteeing that no WAL files are lost even if the standby falls behind.

Managing Replication

Once streaming replication is set up between a primary and one or more standby servers, effective management is necessary to ensure that replication works smoothly and that the standby servers remain in sync with the primary. The replication delay occurs when the standby server falls behind the primary due to high transaction throughput, network latency, or resource limitations on the standby. Conflicts, on the other hand, can happen when read queries on the standby conflict with the replication process, such as when the standby tries to replay WAL changes that affect data currently being queried.

Using the practical setup from the previous section, we will learn how to monitor replication performance, manage delays, and resolve conflicts.

Monitoring Replication Performance

PostgreSQL provides several system views and functions to help track replication health and performance.

Using 'pg_stat_replication'

On the primary server, you can use the **pg_stat_replication** view to monitor the state of replication. This view provides information about connected standby servers, including the replication mode (synchronous or asynchronous), the current WAL position, and any potential lag.

Now, run the following query on the primary server:

```
SELECT
    pid,
    usename AS user,
    application_name AS standby,
    state,
    sync_state,
    write_lag,
    flush_lag,
    replay_lag
FROM
    pg_stat_replication;
```

The **write_lag, flush_lag, replay_lag** columns show the amount of lag at various stages of replication (writing WAL, flushing it to disk, and replaying it on the standby). If any of these values are consistently high, it indicates a replication delay.

Using 'pg_stat_wal_receiver'

On the standby server, the **pg_stat_wal_receiver** view provides details about the WAL receiver process, which handles streaming WAL data from the primary server. It shows the current status of the replication and helps in diagnosing delays.

To do this, run the following query on the standby server:

```
SELECT
    status,
    receive_start_lsn,
```

```
    receive_lsn,
    replay_lsn,
    last_msg_send_time,
    last_msg_receipt_time
FROM
    pg_stat_wal_receiver;
```

Here,

- **receive_lsn**: The last WAL log sequence number (LSN) received from the primary.
- **replay_lsn**: The last WAL LSN that has been replayed on the standby.
- **last_msg_send_time / last_msg_receipt_time**: These columns indicate the time of the last WAL message sent from the primary and received by the standby.

If the difference between **receive_lsn** and **replay_lsn** is significant, it suggests that the standby is falling behind in applying WAL changes, leading to replication delay.

Managing Replication Delays

There are several strategies to mitigate replication delays. Following are:

Adjust WAL Settings

One of the most common causes of replication delays is insufficient WAL retention on the primary server. If the primary server recycles or deletes WAL files before the standby has a chance to process them, the standby will fall behind and require a complete re-sync.

Ensure that the **wal_keep_size** parameter in the primary server's **postgresql.conf** is set to an adequate value:

```
wal_keep_size = 256MB
```

This setting determines how many WAL files the primary should retain to allow the standby to catch up during periods of high transaction activity.

Increase Max WAL Senders and WAL Buffers

If replication is delayed due to resource limitations on the primary server, consider increasing the following parameters:

- max_wal_senders

Controls the maximum number of simultaneous WAL sender processes. If there are many standby servers or a high volume of transactions, increasing this value ensures that enough WAL sender processes are available for replication.

```
max_wal_senders = 10
```

- wal_buffers

Defines the amount of shared memory allocated for WAL data before it's written to disk. Increasing this value can improve replication performance during high transaction volumes.

```
wal_buffers = 16MB
```

Tune Standby for Performance

Replication delays can also occur on the standby server due to insufficient resources, such as CPU, memory, or I/O performance. To optimize the standby server's configuration and assist in reducing the replication lag, following can be done:

- Increase work_mem and shared_buffers

These parameters control the amount of memory used for processing queries and buffering data. Increasing their values allows the standby to process incoming WAL data faster.

```
shared_buffers = 1GB

work_mem = 16MB
```

- Enable read-only queries in parallel

By allowing parallel queries, the standby can handle more read requests while still replaying WAL logs. To enable parallel processing, modify the **max_parallel_workers** and **max_parallel_workers_per_gather** parameters.

```
max_parallel_workers = 4

max_parallel_workers_per_gather = 2
```

Implement WAL Archiving and Retention

If the standby regularly falls too far behind, causing WAL files to be recycled, you may need to implement WAL archiving to ensure that the necessary WAL segments are always available for replication.

To do this, enable WAL archiving and specify an archive command in the **postgresql.conf** file on the primary server:

```
archive_mode = on

archive_command = 'cp %p /path/to/wal_archive/%f'
```

This ensures that even if the standby is temporarily disconnected, the WAL files required to catch up will be saved and available for replay when the standby reconnects.

Handling Replication Conflicts

Replication conflicts occur when the standby server is unable to apply changes because of active queries on the standby. Let us consider if a read query is holding a lock on a table, and the primary tries to replay a **DELETE** operation on that table, the replication will fail until the query is completed.

Monitor Replication Conflicts

You can monitor replication conflicts on the standby server using the **pg_stat_database_conflicts** view:

```
SELECT

    datname,

    confl_lock,

    confl_snapshot,

    confl_bufferpin,

    confl_deadlock

FROM

    pg_stat_database_conflicts;
```

This view shows different types of conflicts:

- **confl_lock**: Conflicts caused by locks held by standby queries.
- **confl_snapshot**: Conflicts due to concurrent transactions trying to access inconsistent data snapshots.
- **confl_bufferpin**: Conflicts caused by buffers pinned by standby queries.

Adjust 'hot_standby_feedback'

To reduce the likelihood of replication conflicts, you can enable **hot_standby_feedback** on the standby server. This setting informs the primary server about the queries running on the standby, preventing the primary from removing rows that are still being queried.

In the standby server's **postgresql.conf**, add the following:

```
hot_standby_feedback = on
```

With this setting enabled, the primary server retains tuples that would otherwise be deleted, reducing the chances of conflicts caused by **DELETE** or **UPDATE** operations on the primary.

Setting Timeout for Conflict Resolution

If conflicts persist and you prefer to prioritize replication over read queries, you can configure a timeout for queries on the standby. This will automatically terminate long-running queries that conflict with WAL replay, allowing replication to proceed.

In the standby server's **postgresql.conf**, set the following parameters:

```
max_standby_streaming_delay = 30s
```

This setting allows queries on the standby to delay replication for a maximum of 30 seconds. After this time, conflicting queries are terminated to prioritize replication.

Failover and Switchover Procedures

In PostgreSQL streaming replication setups, **failover** and **switchover** are two critical procedures used to maintain high availability. **Failover** occurs when the primary server fails unexpectedly, and a standby server is promoted to take over as the new primary. **Switchover**, on the other hand, is a planned process where the roles of the primary and standby servers are switched, often for maintenance purposes or to redistribute load.

Here, we will cover how to **promote a standby server** to a primary server during failover and how to reconfigure your **applications and services** to point to the new primary. We will also cover how to perform a **switchover** procedure to deliberately switch roles between the primary and standby servers.

Failover

Failover occurs automatically or manually when the primary server experiences a failure, and the standby must take over to minimize downtime. In cases where automatic failover isn't configured (or fails), you need to manually promote the standby server to the primary. This involves a few steps to ensure the standby is fully ready to take over as the new primary as below:

Stop the Failed Primary

If the primary server is still running but isn't functioning correctly, stop the PostgreSQL service to prevent further issues:

```
sudo systemctl stop postgresql
```

Promote the Standby Server

On the standby server, use the **pg_ctl** command to promote it to the primary:

```
pg_ctl promote -D /var/lib/postgresql/13/main
```

This command tells the standby server to stop replaying WAL logs and to start accepting write transactions as the new primary.

Verify Promotion

After promoting the standby server, check that it is now running as the primary by querying the **pg_stat_wal_receiver** view, which should no longer be active since the server is no longer in standby mode:

```
SELECT * FROM pg_stat_wal_receiver;
```

If the query returns no rows, it means the server has successfully promoted and is no longer receiving WAL data.

Automatic failover can be configured using third-party tools like **Patroni**, **repmgr**, or **pg_auto_failover**, which monitor the primary server's health and automatically promote a standby when needed. These tools also help in maintaining cluster consistency during failover events.

When a failover occurs, one needs to reconfigure the applications and services to point to the new primary server. Typically, applications are configured to connect to the primary database using a connection string or database URL. After a failover, this connection string must be updated to reflect the new primary server.

Using Virtual IPs (VIPs)

One way to minimize application downtime during failover is to use a **Virtual IP (VIP)** address that points to the current primary server. This way, when failover occurs, you simply need to update the VIP to point to the new primary, and applications won't need to change their connection strings.

- Assign the VIP to the Standby

When the standby server is promoted to primary, assign the VIP to it. This can be done using network commands like **`ip`** or **`ifconfig`**:

```
sudo ip addr add 192.168.1.50/24 dev eth0
```

The VIP (e.g., **`192.168.1.50`**) is now associated with the new primary server.

- Update DNS or Load Balancers

If you are using DNS or a load balancer to direct traffic to the primary server, you'll need to update your DNS entries or load balancer configuration to reflect the new primary's IP address.

Updating Application Connection Strings

If you aren't using VIPs, you'll need to manually update your applications' database connection strings. This can be done in the application's configuration files or environment variables.

For example, if your application was connecting to the old primary using this connection string:

```
jdbc:postgresql://192.168.1.10:5432/titanic_db
```

After failover, change it to point to the new primary:

```
jdbc:postgresql://192.168.1.11:5432/titanic_db
```

Alternatively, if you are using PostgreSQL connection pools like **pgBouncer**, simply reconfigure pgBouncer to connect to the new primary.

Switchover

A **switchover** is a controlled process where the roles of the primary and standby servers are intentionally switched. This is often done for maintenance or load balancing purposes, and it requires careful planning to minimize downtime and ensure data consistency.

Switchover involves demoting the primary server to become a standby and promoting the current standby to become the new primary.

- Stop Write Transactions on the Primary

Before switching roles, ensure that no new write transactions are occurring on the primary. This can be done by briefly stopping the application or setting the database to **read-only mode**:

```
ALTER SYSTEM SET default_transaction_read_only = 'on';

SELECT pg_reload_conf();
```

- Promote the Standby

Promote the standby server to take over as the new primary:

```
pg_ctl promote -D /var/lib/postgresql/13/main
```

- Reconfigure the Old Primary as the New Standby

After promoting the standby, the old primary needs to be reconfigured as a standby server. First, stop the PostgreSQL service on the old primary:

```
sudo systemctl stop postgresql
```

Then, reconfigure it to connect to the new primary by editing **`postgresql.conf`**:

```
primary_conninfo = 'host=192.168.1.11 port=5432
user=rep_user password=rep_password'
```

Finally, start the PostgreSQL service:

```
sudo systemctl start postgresql
```

The old primary will now act as a standby server, replaying WAL logs from the new primary.

Just as in failover, you'll need to update your applications and services to point to the new primary. If you are using a VIP or load balancer, simply update the VIP to point to the new primary.

Otherwise, update your application connection strings manually to reflect the new primary's IP address.

Summary

In summary, we covered the core practical aspects of streaming replication and high availability, with a focus on replication setup, replication management, and failover/switchover. The chapter began by distinguishing between physical and logical replication, as well as introducing the terms synchronous and asynchronous replication. We then went through a hands-on demonstration of setting up streaming replication between a primary and a standby server, configuring replication slots, and ensuring that no data was lost during the replication process. We introduced techniques like hot_standby_feedback and tuning WAL retention settings to optimize replication performance and avoid conflicts.

Finally, we discussed failover and switchover procedures, such as moving a standby server to primary in the event of a failure and switching roles between servers for maintenance purposes. Making use of these techniques, you learn through every step of setting up and maintaining a highly available PostgreSQL system.

CHAPTER 9: POINT-IN-TIME RECOVERY

Brief Overview

In this final chapter, we will go over PostgreSQL's ability to restore databases to a specific historical point using its PITR feature. When it comes to restoring databases following unforeseen incidents like system crashes, accidental data loss, or corruption, this chapter is significant. We start by learning about WAL archiving for PITR, which continuously archives the database's WALs to preserve changes made after each transaction.

Next, we learn to restore the database from a backup and replay the archived WAL files to return it to a specific point in time. These concepts will provide us with a thorough understanding of how PostgreSQL protects data and provides powerful recovery tools for real-world disaster scenarios.

WAL Archiving for PITR

PITR is a powerful feature in PostgreSQL that allows a database to be restored to a specific point in time, rather than just to the time of the last backup. This is especially useful when recovering from unintended changes, such as a mistaken deletion of data or a software bug. PITR works by using a combination of a **base backup** and the **WAL** that record every transaction in the database.

The general process of PITR involves restoring the database from a base backup and then replaying the WAL files generated after the backup to restore the database to the desired state. WAL files are archived to ensure that they can be used for recovery, even if the primary database is no longer accessible. To achieve PITR, you must configure **WAL archiving** on the primary server and properly manage the archived WAL files. This ensures that you can recover your database to any point in time after the base backup, provided the necessary WAL files are available.

Configuring WAL Archiving

To enable PITR in PostgreSQL, the first step is to configure **WAL archiving**. This involves modifying PostgreSQL's configuration file (**`postgresql.conf`**) to ensure that WAL segments are copied to a safe location, such as an external disk or cloud storage, after each transaction. The key parameter that controls WAL archiving is **`archive_command`**, which defines the command that PostgreSQL will execute to archive each WAL file once it is no longer needed for immediate use.

Editing 'postgresql.conf'

To begin, locate and edit the **postgresql.conf** file, typically found in the PostgreSQL data directory (**/etc/postgresql/<version>/main/** on Linux-based systems).

```
sudo nano /etc/postgresql/13/main/postgresql.conf
```

Search for the following parameters and modify them as necessary:

```
archive_mode = on

archive_command = 'cp %p /path/to/wal_archive/%f'

archive_timeout = 60
```

Creating Archive Directory

Next, create the directory where the WAL files will be stored. It is important that this directory is on a secure and reliable storage system, as the WAL files are critical for PITR.

```
sudo mkdir -p /backups/wal_archive/

sudo chown postgres:postgres /backups/wal_archive/

sudo chmod 700 /backups/wal_archive/
```

This directory will store the WAL segments generated after each transaction. Make sure to monitor the available disk space, as WAL files can grow significantly on busy systems.

Testing Archive Command

Before fully enabling WAL archiving, it is a good idea to test the **archive_command** to ensure that WAL files can be successfully copied to the archive location. You can do this by manually copying a WAL file from the **pg_wal** directory to the archive directory:

```
cp
/var/lib/postgresql/13/main/pg_wal/0000000100000000000000
A1 /backups/wal_archive/
```

After running this command, verify that the file was successfully copied:

```
ls -l /backups/wal_archive/
```

If the file appears in the archive directory, the **archive_command** should work as expected when PostgreSQL executes it automatically.

Next, once the **postgresql.conf** file has been modified, restart PostgreSQL to apply the changes:

```
sudo systemctl restart postgresql
```

After the restart, PostgreSQL will begin archiving WAL files as they are generated, using the command specified in **archive_command**.

Managing Archived WAL files

After enabling WAL archiving, the archived WAL files must be managed properly to ensure that they are available for recovery and do not consume excessive storage. Management of WAL files involves ensuring they are stored securely, periodically verifying their integrity, and implementing retention policies to remove old or unnecessary WAL files.

Viewing Archived WAL files

You can verify that WAL archiving is functioning properly by checking the contents of the archive directory:

```
ls -l /backups/wal_archive/
```

You should see a list of WAL files with names like **000000010000000000000A1**, **000000010000000000000A2**, etc. Each file represents a WAL segment that records a portion of the transactions committed to the database.

Implementing Retention Policies

Over time, archived WAL files can consume significant disk space, especially on high-transaction systems. To manage disk usage, you should implement retention policies to remove WAL files that are no longer needed. This can be done manually or using scripts that periodically delete old WAL files.

For example, you can use a simple **cron job** to delete WAL files older than a certain number of days (e.g., 7 days):

```
crontab -e
```

Add the following line to remove WAL files older than 7 days every day at midnight:

```
0 0 * * * find /backups/wal_archive/ -type f -mtime +7 -
exec rm {} \;
```

This command will delete any file in the **/backups/wal_archive/** directory that is older than 7 days. Adjust the retention period to suit your needs based on available storage and recovery requirements.

Verifying WAL file Integrity

It is important to ensure that archived WAL files remain uncorrupted, as they are essential for point-in-time recovery. You can periodically verify the integrity of the WAL files by using the **pg_verify_checksums** tool, which checks for checksum errors in data files:

```
pg_verify_checksums -D /var/lib/postgresql/13/main/
```

This command ensures that the archived WAL files and other data files in the PostgreSQL cluster are intact. If you encounter any errors, you should dig into the issue and consider replacing any corrupted WAL files with a backup copy.

Storing WAL files in a Remote Location

For added security and disaster recovery, it is a good idea to store archived WAL files in a remote location, such as a network-attached storage (NAS) system, cloud storage (e.g., Amazon S3), or a dedicated backup server.

To store WAL files on a remote server, modify the **archive_command** to use a remote copy command such as **scp** or **rsync**. For example, to copy WAL files to a remote backup server:

```
archive_command = 'rsync -a %p
backup_user@backupserver:/backups/wal_archive/%f'
```

This command uses **rsync** to securely transfer each WAL file to a remote server for storage.

Performing Point-in-Time Recovery

PITR is especially useful in situations where a failure or unwanted change occurs, and you need to recover the database to the state it was in just before the event. PITR uses a combination of a **base backup** and the archived **WAL segments** generated after the backup to restore the database.

This section demonstrates how to perform a full **PITR** by first restoring the base backup and then applying WAL segments up to a specific target time.

Restoring from Base Backups

The first step in PITR is restoring the database to the point of the most recent **base backup**. This base backup provides a consistent starting point from which the WAL logs can be replayed to reach the desired recovery point.

Preparing Base Backup

Before initiating the recovery, ensure that the **base backup** is available. This backup is typically created using the **`pg_basebackup`** tool and stored in a backup directory. The base backup contains all the data files and transaction logs needed to start the recovery process.

Suppose the base backup has been stored in **`/backups/base_backup/`**. To restore the backup, the following steps are required:

Stop PostgreSQL Server

To restore the database, first stop the running PostgreSQL instance on the server:

```
sudo systemctl stop postgresql
```

Stopping the server ensures that no new transactions or data modifications occur during the recovery process.

Remove Existing Data Directory

If the data directory already contains an existing database, you must remove it to make way for the restored backup:

```
sudo rm -rf /var/lib/postgresql/13/main/*
```

Be careful when executing this command, as it permanently deletes the current database files. Make sure you have valid backups before proceeding.

Extract Base Backup

Next, restore the base backup into the PostgreSQL data directory. If the base backup is compressed (e.g., in **`.tar.gz`** format), extract it:

```
tar -xzf /backups/base_backup/base.tar.gz -C
/var/lib/postgresql/13/main/
```

This command extracts the base backup to the appropriate data directory.

Prepare WAL Replay

After the base backup is restored, PostgreSQL must be instructed to apply the WAL files to replay the transactions. To do this, you'll need to ensure that the WAL files generated after the base backup are available for recovery.

Copy the archived WAL files from the backup archive directory (in our case, it is **/backups/wal_archive/**) to the PostgreSQL **pg_wal** directory:

```
cp /backups/wal_archive/*
/var/lib/postgresql/13/main/pg_wal/
```

These WAL files will be applied after the base backup to bring the database to the desired state.

Applying WAL Segments

Once the base backup is restored, the next step is to apply the archived WAL segments to the database. These logs contain all the changes that occurred after the base backup was created, and replaying them allows the database to be restored to any point in time.

Setting Recovery Target

To perform **Point-in-Time Recovery**, PostgreSQL needs to know up to which point in time it should replay the WAL logs. This is done by specifying a **recovery target** in a configuration file.

In versions of PostgreSQL prior to 12, this is done in a file called **recovery.conf**. In PostgreSQL 12 and later, you set the recovery parameters directly in **postgresql.conf**, wherein you edit the PostgreSQL configuration file to specify the recovery target. Use a text editor like **nano**:

```
sudo nano /var/lib/postgresql/13/main/postgresql.conf
```

Specify the Recovery Target Time

Add the following lines to specify the recovery target time. Replace **YYYY-MM-DD HH:MM:SS** with the exact time to which you want to recover the database:

```
restore_command = 'cp /backups/wal_archive/%f %p'

recovery_target_time = 'YYYY-MM-DD HH:MM:SS'

recovery_target_action = 'pause'
```

Here,

- **restore_command**: Specifies the command to restore the WAL files from the archive. This command copies the necessary WAL segments from the archive directory to the appropriate location in the PostgreSQL data directory.
- **recovery_target_time**: Defines the exact point in time to which PostgreSQL should replay the WAL logs. You can specify any time after the base backup was taken.
- **recovery_target_action**: Tells PostgreSQL what to do after reaching the recovery target. Setting this to **`pause`** allows you to inspect the state of the database after recovery.

After setting the recovery target, save the changes and close the file.

Starting PITR Process

With the base backup restored and the recovery target time configured, restart the PostgreSQL server to begin the PITR process:

```
sudo systemctl start postgresql
```

Upon startup, PostgreSQL will automatically enter recovery mode and begin replaying the archived WAL logs. The **restore_command** will be executed for each WAL segment, allowing PostgreSQL to apply the changes incrementally.

Monitoring Recovery Process

You can monitor the progress of the recovery by checking the PostgreSQL logs. The logs will indicate which WAL files are being applied and whether any issues have occurred during recovery.

To view the logs:

```
tail -f /var/log/postgresql/postgresql-13-main.log
```

The log file will show messages indicating that PostgreSQL is applying WAL segments, and you will see entries like:

```
LOG:  restored log file "0000000100000000000000A3" from
archive

LOG:  restored log file "0000000100000000000000A4" from
archive
```

These entries confirm that PostgreSQL is successfully replaying the WAL segments. The recovery process continues until all WAL files are applied, or the **recovery_target_time** is reached.

Completing the Recovery

Once the recovery target time is reached, PostgreSQL will pause the recovery process (as specified by **recovery_target_action = 'pause'**). At this point, you can inspect the database to ensure that it has been restored to the correct state.

If you are satisfied with the recovery, finalize the process by allowing PostgreSQL to exit recovery mode and start accepting new transactions. To do this, you can either:

- Change the recovery_target_action to 'promote' in postgresql.conf, or
- Use the pg_ctl promote command:

```
pg_ctl promote -D /var/lib/postgresql/13/main
```

This command promotes the database to the primary mode, allowing it to accept new write transactions. At this point, PITR is complete, and the database is fully operational at the desired point in time.

Verifying the Recovery

Once PostgreSQL has exited recovery mode, it's important to verify that the recovery was successful and that the database is in the correct state.

Check the Database Logs

Review the PostgreSQL logs to ensure there were no errors during recovery. Look for messages indicating that WAL segments were successfully applied and that PostgreSQL has completed recovery.

Run SQL Queries

Run some SQL queries to verify that the data in the database is consistent with the point in time to which you recovered. For example, check that recent transactions are present and that any unwanted changes (e.g., accidental deletions) have been reverted.

```
SELECT * FROM passengers WHERE passenger_id = 1;
```

Check the Recovery Time

Confirm that the database has been restored to the correct recovery target time by querying system views such as **`pg_stat_activity`** or checking the timestamp of recent transactions.

Overall, PITR is an essential tool to recover from accidental data loss or system failures. By archiving WAL files and applying them after restoring a base backup, PostgreSQL allows for flexible and precise recovery to any point in time. The process involves restoring the base backup, applying the archived WAL files, and configuring the recovery target to replay transactions up to the desired time.

Summary

We have now reached the chapter that discussed PITR. As a first step, we established WAL archiving by directing the PostgreSQL server to save all Write-Ahead Logs to an encrypted repository. In order to lay the groundwork for PITR, the chapter continued by showing us how to restore the database from a base backup. Applying the archived WAL files brought the database to the desired point in time after the base backup was restored. This was done by incrementally replaying transactions. To pinpoint precisely when to terminate the recovery process, we made use of recovery_target_time in the configuration file.

We then confirmed that PostgreSQL had left recovery mode and was once again accepting transactions after the database recovery was successful. By examining the database logs and querying the recovered data, we additionally confirmed the recovery's accuracy. In this chapter, we have covered all the bases when it comes to PostgreSQL's PITR functionality, which guarantees data integrity and precise recovery in the event of an accident.

Index

S

T

W

Epilogue

I have successfully completed all the tasks I set out to do in PostgreSQL 17 QuickStart Pro. We have achieved a great deal together. We have upgraded to PostgreSQL 17, and I can confirm that we have ensured exceptional availability and data integrity. From the start, I knew PostgreSQL could be a game-changer in how you approach database management. I am pleased to have completed the entire cycle, chapter by chapter, and to have revealed answers that are applicable in the real world.

I know it can be overwhelming when you're first learning how to set up streaming replication, manage multiple clusters, or fine-tune performance. I am here to reassure you that you can and will overcome these challenges. Now that we have faced these challenges head-on, I am certain you feel the same sense of relief I do, knowing you are fully ready to tackle them on your own. You have the knowledge to maintain the performance, security, and up-to-dateness of your systems. Furthermore, you have the confidence to rapidly identify solutions to any issues that may arise.

Going through point-in-time recovery and backups was absolutely crucial to this strategy. When it comes to worst-case scenarios, it's natural to feel fear. But it's also crucial to understand them. With WAL archiving and recovery techniques, you'll never be caught off guard in a disaster.

You nailed the PostgreSQL 17 command. You can now manage your database environments with ease, ensuring they're highly available and efficient.

Thank You

www.ingramcontent.com/pod-product-compliance
Lightning Source LLC
Chambersburg PA
CBHW080214170726
48282CB00030B/1110
9788119177844